Writing
From Topic to Evaluation

IRIS McCLELLAN TIEDT
Northern Kentucky University

ALLYN AND BACON
Boston London Sydney Toronto

Library of Congress Cataloging-in-Publication Data

Tiedt, Iris M.
  Writing : from topic to evaluation.

  Bibliography: p.
  Includes index.
  1. English language—Composition and
exercises—Study and teaching. 2. Language
arts. 3. Editing. I. Title.
LB1576.T564 1989   428'.007 88-34352
ISBN 0-205-11966-2

Printed in the United States of America
10 9 8 7 6 5 4 3 2 1 93 92 91 90 89

Contents

Preface

The purpose of this handbook is to clarify the questions you and others may have about teaching writing. I have tried to present writing as a way of expressing thinking. It is my belief that students can learn much about writing by reading "with the eye of a writer." I hope that the ideas I share will enable you to re-view the teaching of writing so that it becomes truly exciting.

My intent is to give you a clear explanation of contemporary theories about teaching writing together with sample applications designed to show you exactly how you can put theory into practice. Sample lessons are presented throughout the book—lessons that are fun to teach and that will enable your students to write successfully. All lessons fit the English language arts classroom, but many can be used in work across the curriculum.

Because teachers continue to have questions about teaching students how to edit their writing from first draft to publication, I have developed a sequence of instructional strategies that help you take that "paperload off your back." These ideas will help your students learn how to improve their writing as they work together in pairs and small groups.

One chapter focuses entirely on teaching the conventions, what to teach and how to ensure that instruction is meaningful and effective, not just traditional drill. Various forms of writing are introduced, which will serve as alternatives to the lengthy research paper.

The chapters on evaluation will also answer your questions. Many ways of approaching evaluation are suggested, and I especially emphasize involving students in evaluating their own writing as well as that of other students. Not only is this a good learning strategy for them, but it will save you some time and work. Editing and evaluating writing, as you will see, are closely related processes.

For those who are responsible for staff development, the chapter on holistic scoring shows you exactly how to conduct a training session for teachers. I have provided a full script following the exact procedures I have used with groups of teachers at elementary and secondary levels.

Above all, I hope that I have made teaching writing effectively seem feasible, and that your writing classes will prove enjoyable to you and your students.

Iris Tiedt

1

Teaching Writing: From Topic to Evaluation

People get better at using language when they use it to say things they really want to say to people they really want to say them to, in a context in which they can express themselves freely and honestly.

John Holt

Teaching writing is a complex undertaking, for we never teach writing in isolation. As we consider effective ways of motivating novice writers to put words on paper and then revise and evaluate the writing they have produced, we are talking about the full writing process and about how we teach writing. Furthermore, as we plan a composition lesson, we are also teaching thinking, listening, speaking, and reading skills, for all language skills are inherently interdependent. Writing is a method of expressing ideas about any subject content; it appears in classrooms everywhere and, therefore, must be the concern of every teacher. Clearly, too, teachers and students must be familiar with many types of writing that can be used for widely varied purposes. In this book we will discuss all of these topics.

An effective writing program is student-centered. It engages students in active learning from the selection of the topic to making changes to improve the writing (editing) to evaluating the finished product. Effective writing instruction involves all that we know about effective teaching in general. It is necessarily individualized, beginning at the level where each student is, at any given time, and evaluating progress based on individual achievement. It provides for the growth of each student's self-esteem as students experience success with expressing their thoughts creatively and effectively. It guides students to recognize good writing exemplified in the literature they read and helps students learn to appreciate the authors' thinking, their style of expression, and even how they handle the conventions of expressing ideas in written form. This is the kind of writing program we will envision together as we move through this book.

After reading this chapter, you should be able to:

1. Summarize current thinking about writing instruction

2. Discuss definitions of evaluation and editing

3. Plan a lesson that engages students in expressing thinking through writing

What We Know about Teaching Writing

Contemporary thinking about writing instruction perceives the process of writing as a total learning experience that includes what happens before the student writes (prewriting) and what happens after the student writes (postwriting). During this holistic process, students think, feel, and experience as they produce a piece of writing. *The process itself brings about learning and thus is more important than the end product*—a writing selection that we might grade. How can we evaluate the total writing process? That is the problem we will address together in this book.

In planning a writing program for students at K–14 (junior college) levels, we follow a model that begins with a strong oral language and thinking base and progresses through experiences with varied forms of writing, as shown in Figure 1–1.

This model presents writing as a complex of skills that is directly and inextricably tied into the total language and literacy development of a student. Presenting writing as a way of learning that never occurs devoid of content also leads to presenting writing as "thinking." Writing is one way of expressing what we think. There-

Figure 1–1. Tiedt Holistic Model for Teaching Writing

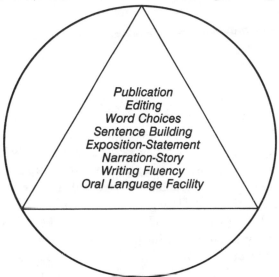

Source: Tiedt/Bruemmer/Lane/Stelwagon/Watanabe/Williams, *Teaching Writing in K–8 Classrooms: The Time Has Come,* © 1983 Prentice Hall, p. 11. Reprinted by permission of Prentice Hall, Inc., Englewood Cliffs, New Jersey.

fore, writing skills should grow along with learning and thinking in every classroom.

Through working with teachers in the California Writing Project[1] and sharing the experiences and thinking of other instructors who are developing approaches to composition instruction across the country, we have gained certain basic understandings about the writing process. These understandings provide the foundation on which this entire book is based.

Students learn to write by writing.

No sixteen-year-old learns to drive a car by talking about driving or viewing films about driving. Sooner or later, he or she has to sit in the driver's seat and move the car cautiously onto the highway. In the same way, students must write, creating different forms, speaking to varied audiences, and experimenting with interesting

stylistic devices. Instruction and guidance will introduce new information, but the student writer must apply it in a real-life situation—truly a "hands-on" experience.

Writing expresses thinking.

Language and thinking develop together from birth. Exercis-
ing amazing thinking powers, young Carlos abstracts the basic
structures of grammar in the language surrounding him. Soon he
creates a simplified "child grammar," and very rapidly he produces
sentences that are almost as complex and fully expanded as those
that adults use. Without teacher or parental instruction and pressure, the child enthusiastically practices talking, learning new concepts, and adding vocabulary. We can observe the thinking that is
growing by listening to the child's audible performance in words.

At the age of five, Carlos arrives in school with a wealth of
knowledge and abilities. This prior knowledge and practice with
thinking is a valuable asset. We need to make Carlos aware of what
he knows (metacognition) and to show him how to apply his knowledge and abilities to the tasks of reading and writing. From the
beginning days in school, Carlos needs to recognize that he has ideas
and that what he thinks is important; we choose strategies that build
his self-esteem, encouraging him to express these ideas confidently
in writing.

In teaching writing we guide students to see the relationships
between thinking and writing processes. We note these relationships as we apply this Writing "Thinking" Model (Figure 1–2) which
leads students to collect data, to process it, and to publish it. These
developmental stages coincide with prewriting, writing, and
postwriting.

Following this model, students collect information, process it
in some manner, and then present it to others. Data collection, as
can be seen, is fundamental to all thinking operations.

Students learn to write by reading.

As students observe reading either visually or aurally, they
begin to internalize just what writing is and the forms that it can
take. They observe how the writer presents ideas, uses language in

Figure 1–2. A Writing "Thinking" Model for Instruction

Stage 1: Data Collecting

Experiencing
Exploring
Observing
Questioning
Brainstorming
Experimenting
Listing
Recording

Stage 2: Data Processing

Categorizing
Comparing
Evaluating
Imagining
Connecting
Synthesizing

Stage 3: Data Publishing

Discussing
Composing
Forming
Communicating
Reviewing
Integrating
Transforming

Source: Iris M. Tiedt et al., *Teaching Thinking in K–12 Classrooms* (Boston: Allyn and Bacon, 1989).

imaginative ways, and structures sentences for effect. They may even notice the use of punctuation and capitalization or the spelling of unusual words. Students learn to write by reading.

Before we expect students to produce a specific form of writing, it is important that they observe how authors write that form. They need to become acquainted with the features of a fairy tale or of a book review before they can write one successfully. We must plan lessons that expose students to an ever expanding variety of types of writing modeled in literature by the best of writers. Students also learn to write by reading writing done by other students, for they, too, provide models that demonstrate aspects of writing from which young writers can learn.

Writing is not easy.

Of all the language skills, writing is the most difficult; it is hard work. As with speaking, the writer generates the ideas. Carlos is thinking about something and wants to express what he is thinking. The natural first step, an easy one, is to verbalize what he is thinking. The problems arise only when he begins to use the written language, for he is then faced with spelling, the many arbitrary conventions we have for presenting thoughts in writing (mechanics), and the physical labor of writing each word—a much slower process than speaking directly to his audience. We teachers must recognize the difficulty of the writing tasks we assign students.

Our job is to remove as many obstacles as possible, to facilitate what the student is trying to do. We encourage students to talk before they write, so they think out what they want to say. We show them techniques for beginning to organize their thoughts, for example, clustering their ideas on paper. We tell them to forget spelling and the mechanics at first while they write freely, using invented spellings, to capture exciting ideas before they escape. We also introduce them to word processing to facilitate the labor of revising. We select evaluation strategies that are nonthreatening and realistic. What we do as teachers is crucial to the success of a writing program and to the success of each student.

Writing can be taught.

Students can learn to write more effectively. We provide a model of an adult writing as we work with them during writing workshops, sharing the problems we have in writing. We introduce concepts formally, for example, telling students about metaphor, sharing examples, and having them compose metaphors. We also help students become aware of literature as writing as they learn to "read like writers." We make students aware that the writing they read is "thinking" expressed in written language.

We can engage students in identifying the qualities of good writing and establishing criteria for judging the success of their own writing. Students who participate in a well-designed writing program are motivated to try specific ideas that will make their writing more effective and more interesting to the peers who comprise their audience.

Writing is a way of learning in all classrooms.

Students who are dealing with ideas, the content in any subject area, will use writing as a way of expressing their thoughts. Teachers across the curriculum need to know writing forms appropriate to their fields—a variety that includes more than just the research paper. Teachers also need to develop realistic expectations for writing as a way of learning and to discover how to create criteria for each writing activity with their students. English teachers can reach across the curriculum to help other teachers integrate languaging skills into all departmentalized classrooms and elementary teachers can readily reinforce language development throughout the day in a self-contained classroom. Teachers need to see writing as a way of communicating thought in any subject area. Emphasis should be placed on ideas expressed through writing in the history or biology class rather than the teaching of writing that might occur in an English class.

SUMMARY

We perceive writing as one way of expressing thinking— a performance process. Students should write frequently and they should recognize literature as an example of a real person's writing. In order to achieve this goal, we teachers must provide models that our students can try to emulate. All of the sources from which these understandings are drawn, listed at the end of the chapter, are well worth reading in more detail. These understandings about the writing process and writing instruction provide a new perspective of writing for K–12 curriculum which should shape our teaching. Implementation of these ideas in curriculum development should lend new life to teaching and to learning and should certainly strengthen writing programs. Preparing teachers at all levels who can carry out such exciting programs is a crucial step toward achieving effective educational reform.

An outstanding writing program exemplifies the following quality indicators:

1. Students write frequently during the school day, using writing to organize and to express their thinking.

2. Students see a purpose for writing as they speak to different audiences about topics and issues that concern them.

3. Students take responsibility for their writing as they engage in editing and evaluating their own writing and that of other students.

4. Evaluation of student writing is individualized based on individual progress and potential.

5. Reading is clearly connected to the writing process.

6. Good writing is honored in the school and community.

Designing Writing Instruction

Well-designed writing lessons, including subject content lessons that utilize writing as a way of learning, reflect current thinking about the writing process and about teaching. Such lessons demonstrate concern for the individual student's abilities and motivation. They include such recognized strategies as modeling, active learning, and integrated instruction. An effective writing lesson will be comprised of these major components:

Objectives

Prewriting stimulus

Writing stimulus

Postwriting follow-up

Evaluation based on objectives

CLARIFYING OBJECTIVES FOR INSTRUCTION

As we focus on the writing process, just what are our objectives as we plan a writing lesson? Clearly, we must be concerned equally about cognitive and affective objectives if learning is to take place. We must also bring in all that we know of current learning theory to help us determine good practice. Notice that error avoidance is not our primary goal. Our list of outcomes might well begin with these, phrased in terms of what we expect students to be able to do.

Students will:

See themselves as writers

Engage in writing freely and positively

Develop fluency (ease) in writing

Discuss thinking as an integral part of writing

Realize that what they think is important

Write for diverse audiences

Listen to the writing of other students

Define purposes for writing

Experience varied forms of writing

Observe literature selections as examples of writing

Participate in transactions with *other* authors

Establish criteria for good writing (rubrics)

Apply these criteria to their own writing and that of others

Write with increasing ease and effect

Write in all curricular areas

Experiment with various stylistic devices

Identify grammatical structures in English sentences

Increase knowledge of word meanings (vocabulary)

Follow common conventions of usage

Utilize conventions of punctuation and capitalization

Discuss concepts about language

Spell English words with reasonable accuracy

Edit some writing to a final draft

Make selected writings public

Use a word processor for writing

Express pride in their writing achievement

As we plan schoolwide composition programs or as we plan a lesson for a single classroom, we need to begin with the objectives—what we want students to know and which learning experiences will benefit them. The objectives we select may guide us to read aloud Frank O'Connor's "First Confession" to stimulate discussion followed by writing a childhood memory, or Paul Zindel's *I Love My Mother* to illustrate the interesting use of repetition to form a pattern that students can emulate.

This list includes both specific and general outcomes. The broader objectives can be broken down into more specific items, the focus of one or more lessons. Obviously, experimenting with stylistic devices will be the objective for many lessons that might focus on, for example, parallelism, metaphor, or alliteration. And, of course, one lesson will probably meet several objectives, for instance, increasing fluency, developing a positive attitude toward writing, and teaching the use of quotation marks in a dialogue.

It is also important to note that the outcomes specific to writing fit easily with objectives for any content area. For example, a history lesson might be designed to meet these objectives.

Students will:

1. Analyze Franklin's role as Minister to France

2. Write a conversation between Franklin and Lafayette

3. Establish criteria for evaluating the writing

4. Revise the writing in pairs

Presenting all literature to students as writing done by real people encourages them to engage in transactions with authors. Seeing the writing as the "thinking" of that person will make it natural for students to question, to agree or disagree, and to express their own thinking in writing. Thus, we can guide students to think independently and to assume responsibility for their own learning.

PROVIDING A PREWRITING STIMULUS

Everything that precedes a particular writing experience can be thought of as the prewriting stimulus. The child's experiences— playing at home with older brothers, traveling with the family, visiting the zoo—all add to the student's store of knowledge. Concept development, vocabulary, self-esteem, and many other factors influence each student's performance on any writing task. What a student brings to the task, his or her prior knowledge, is something over which we have no control and which we cannot assess clearly. We must, however, consider the student's prior knowledge as we plan writing lessons, and we must show students how to draw on this knowledge to advantage.

Therefore, we begin composition lessons with a prewriting warm-up to ascertain that the writing activity will have meaning for each student. We encourage talk, the sharing of ideas, as the motors warm up, getting ready to take off. As part of this prewriting experience, we write words and phrases on the board to lend support to the students' independent writing. We may introduce a brainstorming device, such as clustering or the Venn diagram, to help students organize their thoughts. These prewriting activities help students bring out ideas pertinent to the topic at hand. We continuously reinforce the understanding that each student possesses many good ideas and that what he or she says is important.

Prewriting activities tend to be oral. They involve listening, speaking, and, above all, thinking. The activities should be designed to extend student thinking. The stimuli from which a teacher can select are varied:

Short books: *I Can't Said the Ant*; *The Giving Tree*

Parts of novels: Chapter 1 of *The Good Earth*

Short stories: "The Lady or the Tiger"

Poems: "I Hear America Singing"; "You Come, Too"

Short films: *My Old Man*; *Stringbean*

Pictures: Posters; calendars; small magazine illustrations

Inanimate objects: John Hancock's pen; students' desks

Events: First snowfall; a hurricane or earthquake

Art objects: *Mona Lisa*; *The Thinker*

Magazine articles: "How to . . ."; "Travels in . . ."

Games: "Hangman"; *Monopoly*; soccer

ENGAGING STUDENTS IN A WRITING ACTIVITY

After the prewriting stimulus, we move into the writing activity—
the performance by the student. We try to engage students in writing a wide variety of forms, including both prose and poetry. Some
of the forms of discourse appropriate for student writing include:

Directions

Stories (narration)

  anecdote
  personal essay
  fable
  pourquoi tale
  tall tale
  fairy tale
  short story

Letters

  request
  friendly
  opinion

Journals

Diaries

Logs

Drama
> skit
> role play
> monologue
> duologue

Poetry
> narrative
> haiku
> free verse

Reviews
> book or film
> television

Report
> expository paragraph
> essay
> article
> research paper

Before asking students to write a specific form, we introduce the structure by showing examples. The students need to develop a "sense of story" before writing a story and, in the same way, they need to hear and to read other forms in order to create them. This sense of form, part of the students' knowledge of the world, *schema theory*, enables a writer to create specific genres. This information is usually presented as part of the prewriting experience, often by the teacher reading aloud to the students, introducing varied forms of writing. Students also meet different schemata (singular: schema) as they read. Thus, over a period of time, students develop a repertoire of forms they can write.

PLANNING FOR POSTWRITING FOLLOW-UP

The postwriting activity is anything that follows the students' writing—sharing, editing, or publishing. It can be any of the paired or small-group editing activities discussed in Chapters 3 and 4.

Postwriting activities include evaluation of the writing. Any of these activities may be done individually, in pairs, in small groups, in the large group, or in teacher-student conferences.

EVALUATING THE LESSON

The final component of a lesson based on the full writing process is evaluation of the lesson. Did we achieve the objectives that we defined before planning the lesson to meet those objectives? This kind of evaluation may take many forms:

Observation of student participation

Student summary of achievement

Collection of student work to diagnose individual problems

Examination of individual student portfolios

Student analysis of the writing process in logs or journals

Conferencing with another student or the teacher

Teacher participation in group activities

Report made orally or in writing by groups

Checkpoint reports individually or by groups

Evaluation of a lesson can be done by the teacher, individual students, or a group of students. Preferably, it will be the responsibility of everyone in the class.

We must give students frequent opportunities to engage in evaluation (thinking) activities. A good way to end any class is to discuss "What did we achieve today?" Students may write a few sentences to answer the question, "What did I learn today?" Thus, students are conscious that learning did take place, *as expected.* The students are also well-prepared to reply to the parental query "What did you do in school today?" Such metacognitive exercises guide students to becoming reflective thinkers who are fully engaged in the learning process.

A LESSON PLAN

Included here is a form for planning lessons following the process just described. You may wish to duplicate copies for use in planning writing lessons that engage students in integrating thinking, listening, speaking, reading, and writing as described in the preceding pages. Your lessons will move students through the total writing process from prewriting (data collection), to writing (data processing), and then to postwriting (data publishing), including evaluation. Following is one example of a lesson that you might create using this format.

A SAMPLE LESSON

TITLE: From Observation into Poetry

LEVEL: Grades 2–12

OBJECTIVES:

Students will:

1. Collect data based on observation

2. Organize their data into a poem

3. Share their writing in small groups

4. Begin developing an "I can" attitude toward writing

PROCEDURES:

This is a good beginning activity for a new group of students. It can be used successfully with a large group of people.

Prewriting Stimulus (Data Collecting)

Ask students to take out a pen or pencil. Tell them that you want them to observe this ordinary object to see how much information they can collect about it in a short time. Direct them to jot down words or phrases (not sentences) as you slowly suggest the following:

1. What does this writing instrument look like? Jot down words or phrases that say something about its appearance—color, shape, size.

2. Now think about how it feels. Write some words that tell about its texture, perhaps its warmth or coolness, or what it feels like.

3. What other senses can we use? Does it have a smell? Can it make sounds? Do you associate any taste with it?

4. What about this pen or pencil's history? Where did it come from? What experiences might it have had? Use your imagination, if you like.

5. Does anyong else have ideas we might consider? Encourage students to offer suggestions like the following:

   What can it do, its function?

   How do you feel about it?

   What are its parts?

   How reliable is it?

   Does it have personality?

Walk around the room as students respond to each idea. After students have had ample time to record notes about each idea, move on to the writing activity.

Writing Activity (Data Processing)

Now that you have collected ideas about this worthy writing instrument, you are going to write an ode praising it, extolling its value. An ode usually begins with the word *oh*, and it might proceed something like this example:

Oh, wonderful communicator of knowledge,
I salute you.
You inspire me to think great thoughts
As I sit at my desk alone in the cool evening.

Read the example aloud. Note that the writer uses the first person, I, and is speaking to the pen. Then remove the example and direct students to begin their first line by writing *Oh* and addressing their pen or pencil. Encourage them to use humor and imagination.

Postwriting Follow-Up (Data Publishing)

After students have had time to write a number of lines (even if they are not finished), direct the class to divide into groups of four to six. Each student will read what he or she has written aloud to the group, and the group is then to select one of the odes to share with the whole class.

As time permits, discuss features of some of the best writing that made it effective. Students may complete their odes in class or as homework. The completed odes can be displayed on a large bulletin board or stapled together with an attractive cover prepared by one of the class members. Following are several examples of this type of ode written in a writing workshop.

Oh, pen of mine,
So sleek and fine,
Black to the letter—
Could an instrument be better?
Quick of temper,
Slim in design,
I'm grateful that you are mine.
Drawing, communicating,
Making a point,
Of single construction
With nary a joint!
Reliable, I hope,
'Til the day is through.
Oh, Black Pilot Pen—
A toast to you!
                    Gail Bernardo

O! tapered silver bullet,
Used to give my thoughts to posterity,
How soundlessly you move across the barren, yellow paper.
With lines and dots and circles
You bring context to my mind's eye
And force logic to my thinking.

What once I found silent, waxtipped,
Among a box of twelve duplicates
Now separates itself to find a personality in mine.
You now are different from the rest
For I have carried you to experience—
Lost you for a time in my desk,
Sent you clattering across the floor.

You and I are now the same,
Made unique by chance acquaintance.

                                        Joanna French

Oh, mechanical friend,
You have saved me from madness
So many times

The teacher drones on:
    "Class, today we are going to write
    An expository essay."
I click you in time to the music
In my soul.
    "Stop that clicking, whoever's doing that!"
Let's take you apart, my friend.
One twist, two.
Ahh! There!
    A cartridge,
    A spring.
Now if I keep my hands under the table
I can play with these parts.

There is no record of the many pens
I have taken apart.
If I had only known that school would be so boring,
I'd have kept a record of the number of
Ballpoint pens that have saved me from madness,
And I'd now be in the
Guiness Book of World Records!

                                        Jane Birenbaum

EVALUATION:

Have students write a response to this activity in their learning logs. Suggest that they note what they learned from experiencing this lesson. Compare their responses with the objectives for the lesson.

SUMMARY

This overview of the writing process sets the stage for our more detailed discussion of editing and evaluating student writing. Before proceeding, it is important that the reader recognize the following:

> Teaching writing is more than just assigning a topic and letting students write. The effective teacher of writing assumes responsibility for motivating, planning writing experiences, developing rapport with the group to facilitate editing and evaluation, extending experiential backgrounds to supply content for writing activities, and perhaps, most important, appreciating the results of student efforts.[2]

How Evaluating and Editing Writing Are Related

As illustrated in the discussion of the writing process, both evaluation and editing of student writing occur while and after the student writes. Both processes are recursive, seldom following clear linear procedures. Involving students in both processes provides a valuable learning experience for all. Students begin to discover just what good writing can be.

 We teachers play a crucial role in planning composition instruction that offers students opportunities to learn how to edit and evaluate their own writing. We should *never serve as copy editors*. This traditional practice is defeating for students and engages teachers in a time-consuming, thankless task—enough to discourage anyone from teaching composition. A primary goal of this book is to describe just how we can teach writing more effectively and, at the same time, more enjoyably.

First, let us define the terms we are using and consider just how editing and evaluation are related.

EVALUATING STUDENT WRITING

The emphasis in evaluation should be on its root meaning, *value*, a positive perspective that stresses the worth of each student's writing. We can assume that there is worth in every piece of student writing and, on the other hand, that each student has room for growth or improvement—learning that will add value to his or her writing. We need to recognize that writing is very personal and that exposing one's thinking on paper means taking risks. Student writers need reassurance, acceptance, and appreciation as they express their thinking in writing for others to see. Editing and evaluation processes must be planned with care so as to nurture, rather than kill, beginning writing efforts.

Grading, in contrast to evaluation, is equated with ranking according to set standards (for example, a prime cut of beef compared to commercial grade). We grade students and report these grades on report cards: A, B, C, D, F; or Superior, Excellent, Good, Average, Poor; or Satisfactory, Unsatisfactory. We grade students and their work, but we seldom spell out the criteria used to determine these grades. Through the traditional practice of grading and issuing report cards, we have taught students to focus on grades rather than the value of their achievements. We can improve grading practices by focusing on the values of students' work, by identifying the quality indicators required for each grade.

All teachers have at times read a set of student papers, then tossed them in piles—outstanding work, totally inadequate work, and papers that fell in the middle. This middle group was then sorted into a finer selection of those that fell above the average and those that fell below. In the end, the papers were sorted according to some internalized ideas about what makes good writing. Clarifying these criteria and sharing them with other teachers, making them explicit, and talking about them with students leads to better teaching and increased learning. If "grading" is to be done, students should be involved in the process. This process provides a learning experience for the students and lightens the teacher's workload.

When it is necessary to put a grade on the students' report cards, students can help make these decisions. We need to consider student performance in two ways.

- First, we should take a writing sample, a benchmark, at the beginning of the year to see just how well each individual writes. Periodically, other writing samples can be compared to the original benchmark to see how much the individual student has grown.

- Second, we do need to report to students and their parents how well each student performs according to a set of standards based on realistic expectations for students of that age.

Thus, we allow for individualization of instruction, including evaluation, as well as the achievement of reasonable proficiency or competency levels. And we invite students to participate in self-evaluation, which is an important thinking process.

THE EDITING PROCESS

Editing is a broad term that can be defined generally as "what an editor does." Editing is *more than proofreading*. A good writer learns to edit his or her own writing, rethinking and reshaping it before *making it public*, that is, sending it off to a publisher.

We can teach students how to edit their own writing, as well as that of other student writers, before the writing is "published" (displayed on the bulletin board, included in a class collection of writings, sent to the editor of the local newspaper). Teaching editing techniques focuses on the craft of writing.

Editing in a classroom is similar to, but different from, editing by a commercial publisher. In a large publishing house, the editorial process is handled by several people—the general editor who handles "conceptual editing or ideas," the line editor who focuses on literary quality "line by line," and the copy editor who cleans up the mechanics and marks the manuscript for the printer. All of these editors work directly with the author at each stage of development. Editor Kathleen Anderson contrasts editing in a publishing house with editing done in a classroom, thus:

> Editing in the classroom is not as businesslike. A teacher does not have to be as selective about the material a student writes nor does the work have to be letter perfect. It is more important for teachers to guide and incite their students' imaginations, exciting them about imaginative uses of language. The classroom should be seen as a birthing room where new life is formed in an atmosphere of mutual support.[3]

Editing, as part of teaching writing (discussed in more detail in Chapters 3 and 4), is comprised of several steps:

Step 1:   Reading and rereading (orally and silently)

Step 2:   Revision: Rethinking, Reshaping, Rewriting (several drafts)

Step 3:   Final Copy (written in ink, set in type, or printed with the computer)

Step 4:   Proofreading (to catch surface errors in final copy)

Step 5:   Publication

This editing process begins with the individual writer who is supported by fellow student editors and the teacher as editor. Although presented in a chronological sequence, all aspects of editing can occur at any time during the writing process. However, all steps should be reviewed as the final draft of a polished piece of writing is being completed. Notice that the student writer must assume responsibility for editing his or her own work. The teacher, however, sets up situations that call for small-group editing and arranges conferences with individual students to provide editorial support.

Not everything that a student writes will be edited fully, as described. If students write daily in all classes, the writing will be for varied purposes—note taking, recording transactions in a reading log, engaging in a written conversation with another student, and so on. All writing, however, will be stored in individual student portfolios as evidence of writing that has been done by each student. Thus, the portfolio contains a developmental record of a student's writing accomplishments for perhaps one marking period. At that time students can sort and arrange their writing selections to present as a collection of their writing to be assessed with the teacher. The portfolio is invaluable as evidence for parents of what each student has achieved.

Although there is not enough time or the need to edit all writing, we will periodically schedule a significant writing activity that demands full editing. Students do learn much about thinking and improving their writing as they engage in the full editing process. As they edit, they are applying the identified quality indicators for good writing.

HOW EVALUATING AND EDITING WRITING ARE RELATED

As we talk with students about editing their writing, polishing it before making it public, we necessarily begin defining the characteristics of good writing (evaluation). We begin making a list of what the good writer does, based on what these young writers know. The following is an example:

A good writer:

Uses capital letters at the beginning of sentences

Writes sentences that flow

Spells words right

Paints a picture that you can see

Doesn't repeat the same word too many times

The list grows with the class, becoming more specific and more sophisticated as the students learn more about writing. For instance, students may observe in literature that they read how effective the repetition of a word or idea can be, and sooner or later, they may revise the final item on the list. Displayed on the classroom wall, this set of guidelines assists students as they edit their work. In the same way, the checklist can be used to evaluate student writing.

We can also think of evaluating and editing in terms of who is involved—the individual student, groups of students, or teacher-student combinations. Table 1–1 illustrates another way of relating editing and evaluating. Notice that the two processes support each other, and they may occur at the same time. We make judgments that lead to revision, and revision has the purpose of producing more effective writing.

Students can evaluate their own writing and improve it by working alone. They can also work with other students in pairs, response groups of four to six students, or in the large group comprising the entire class. Students will work with the teacher in a variety of ways—an individual conference, a small-group learning situation, and full-class instruction. Such approaches to editing and evaluating writing are described in the following chapters of this book.

The important thing about both editing and evaluating student writing is that the students be directly involved. Students need to know what constitutes "good writing," writing that is good enough to receive an outstanding mark. They should know specific ways to improve their writing: organizational techniques, vocabulary to aid elaboration, stylistic devices, and so on. Students should know before they begin to write which criteria will be used to evaluate their

Table 1–1. Editing and Evaluating Writing

Self	Peer Group	Teacher/ Student(s)
Self-assessment (Read aloud)	Pair cooperation	Conference with one student
Use of tape recorder (Record and listen)	Response group collaboration	Small-group seminar
Use of reference tools	Whole-group learning	Whole-class instruction

work. These criteria serve as guidelines for the successful completion of a writing activity. Of course, in order to communicate these ideas about editing and evaluation to students, we have to clarify our own knowledge and thinking.

SUMMARY

Student writers will benefit from positive evaluation of their work. Therefore, we begin by assessing and accepting the students' writing as it exists at any one time, recognizing that all writers can improve their knowledge of the craft. We then set up our classroom as an ongoing research study by taking a writing sample—a benchmark—from each student in our study. Gradually, we introduce information and techniques that lead students to write with greater effect, using selected intervention strategies. Individualized instruction provides help for students of all ability levels in a class. Students learn to write through reading and editing the work of other students, and they learn what good writing is as they establish criteria for the successful completion of each writing task they undertake. Editing and evaluation work hand in hand in a student-centered writing workshop facilitated by an informed instructor.

We show our students how to edit and evaluate writing with their peers, which provides multiple benefits for our students. This approach also removes the paperload from our backs, thereby freeing us to spend more time teaching. At the end of the instructional period, we take another writing sample to compare with the original benchmark. Both the teacher and each individual student will take pride in the achievement that has been made.

Reflection

Writing is a complex process that involves students in thinking from the time they conceive an idea to the final polishing of the revised manuscript. Students learn to structure sentences as they listen to language around them, and they learn how language is written by reading the work of their peers as well as published writing. Like speaking, writing is a productive process; unlike speaking, however, writing is fairly slow and involves the use of motor skills that may not be well developed. Writing also demands the use of conventions such as punctuation, capitalization, and spelling, as well as standard usage. These obstacles make writing the most difficult of the language arts.

Yet, writing can also be a very exciting, rewarding process. It is our job as teachers to show students how to minimize the difficulties and to guide them to recognize and to appreciate their achievements. The ideas presented in this text are designed for teachers who want to improve their writing programs and to provide their students with successful, enjoyable writing experiences.

Challenge

At the end of each chapter, we suggest ways that you can begin working with the information presented in the chapter.

1. Plan a writing lesson following the Process Model described in the first part of this chapter. Use a short piece of literature as the stimulus, for example, one of the following books:

   The Giving Tree by Shel Silverstein
   And Now We Are a Family by Judith Meredith
   I Love My Mother by Paul Zindel
   Outside Over There by Maurice Sendak
   A Tree Is Nice by Janice Udry

   For older students, select short stories, for example:

   "My Oedipus Complex" by Frank O'Connor
   "Charles" by Shirley Jackson
   "All Summer in a Day" by Ray Bradbury

2. Brainstorm a list of all the different kinds of writing that might occur in a particular class—one that you teach, if possible. Share your list with others in a small group. Add

other ideas that are suggested so that you have an extensive list from which to choose writing activities.

3. Ask a group of students how they feel about having their writing evaluated. Discuss how they would evaluate student writing if they were teachers.

Endnotes

1. For ten years the author was Director of the South Bay Writing Project at San Jose State University, one of the nineteen centers of the California Writing Project.

2. Iris M. Tiedt. *The Language Arts Handbook.* Englewood Cliffs, NJ: Prentice-Hall, 1983, p. 177.

3. Kathleen Anderson. "Editing: The Teaching of Craft." *Teachers & Writers* (March-April 1986):8.

Exploring Further

Look for such books as the following to find out more about editing and evaluating student writing.

Bereiter, Carl, and Scardamalia, Marlene. *The Psychology of Written Composition.* Erlbaum, 1987.
California State Department of Education. *Handbook for Planning an Effective Writing Program,* 3rd ed. The Department, 1986. An excellent inexpensive overview of the writing process; recommended practices; 72 pp.
Hillocks, George, Jr. *Research on Written Composition: New Directions for Teaching.* National Conference on Research in English/ERIC, 1986. A much-needed assessment of research on writing at all levels; available from NCTE.
Jensen, Julie, ed. *Composing and Comprehending.* National Council of Teachers of English, 1985. An excellent collection of articles

that summarize contemporary thinking about teaching the English language arts.

Kahn, Elizabeth et al. *Writing about Literature*. National Council of Teachers of English, 1984. Part of Theory into Practice Series; ideas for helping students write successfully; 54 pp.

Myers, Miles, and Gray, James. *Theory and Practice in the Teaching of Composition: Processing, Distancing, and Modeling*. National Council of Teachers of English, 1983. Twenty-two essays that illustrate three approaches to writing; 256 pp.

North, Stephen M. *The Making of Knowledge in Composition*. Boynton-Cook, 1987.

Parker, Robert, and Goodkin, Vera. *The Consequences of Writing: Enhancing Learning in the Disciplines*. Boynton-Cook, 1987.

Shuman, R. Baird, ed. *Education in the 80's: English*. National Education Association, 1981. Twenty-one short chapters focusing on various aspects of English language arts teaching; good overview of concerns in the field.

Smith, Michael. *Reducing Writing Apprehension*. National Council of Teachers of English, 1984. Suggests teaching practices designed to reduce student fears; 40 pp.

Strunk, William, Jr., and White, E. B. *The Elements of Style*, 3rd ed. Macmillan, 1979. A summary of information about writing that will help any teacher; 85 pp.

Tiedt, Iris M. et al. *Teaching Writing in K–8 Classrooms*. Prentice-Hall, 1983. Describes a full writing program beginning with oral foundations; includes chapters on editing and evaluation of student writing; applicable at all levels; 257 pp.

2

Designing a Student-Centered Writing Program

It's not often that someone comes along who is a true friend and (teaches us to be) a good writer.

E. B. White

A strong writing program is part of the total English language arts program, for writing is never taught in isolation. Thus, as we begin to focus on evaluating the writing program, we soon find that we need to consider the whole English program. Furthermore, effective evaluation of student writing begins with the basics of good teaching, for how we teach reflects our general attitude toward students, our knowledge of student interests, and our concern for their abilities. Evaluation provides the foundation for planning a writing program, for it goes back directly to the goals and objectives we have spelled out for student learning. An effective writing program must be student-centered, and it must integrate language arts instruction.

In this chapter we will explore the relationship of curriculum and evaluation to determine directions that you can take in your own school setting. We also point out the importance of teacher and student cooperative planning in creating a strong writing program. We provide guidelines that will aid you in carrying out program development in your school or district.

After reading this chapter, you should be able to:

1. Describe the features of a strong writing program

2. Discuss the relationship of the writing program to the total English language arts curriculum

3. Enumerate student needs as learners

4. Support student involvement in curriculum development

5. Suggest ways to engage students in evaluating their own writing and the writing of others

Planning a Schoolwide Writing Program

Since you are reading this book, you probably want to improve your writing program. It is also likely that you are interested in learning more about the evaluation of student writing. That seems like a fair assumption about you and your intentions, but we can make no such assumptions about the other teachers or administrators in your school. For that reason, we must depend on you to share information and to initiate planning that might result in a more effective writing program for the students, as well as the teachers, in your school.

GETTING STARTED

Let's begin by thinking about the teachers in your school or district who are recognized as good teachers of writing. Jot down answers to such questions as the following:

1. Who are the teachers who teach writing? (Be as specific as possible, listing names, if known. Some of these persons may teach subjects other than English language arts.)

2. How great is the need for improving composition instruction in your district? in your school? Have there been any recent assessments of writing that provide scores you can cite?

3. Do you feel strongly enough about this need to do something about it?

4. Which teachers share your concerns? With whom could you form a committee to plan strategies for improving your composition program?

Plan your tactics carefully. Start by making a few nonthreatening telephone calls, beginning with someone you're pretty sure you can count on for support. For example, say:

I'm concerned about our writing program. The student test scores are much lower than they should or could be. What do you think?

Assuming an affirmative response, you can continue:

What can *we* do about it? (Pause for sharing.) I've been making a list of teachers who might work with us. (Add names to the list as you talk together.) Do you think we could get them to come to an exploratory meeting?

Move on this immediately. Set a date, time, and place, and divide up the names of persons to be contacted. Phoning is quick and it permits you to ask for an immediate commitment. If you are dealing with the whole district, you may need more help with calling, and political wisdom demands that key curriculum personnel be involved from the beginning. You may also want to see that each school is represented. Also be sure to include several superior English language arts students from different levels on the planning team.

PLANNING TOGETHER

Before the meeting you may want to share information with the members of the group who have agreed to attend. You might duplicate copies of an article about teaching writing that presents your point of view succinctly. The National Council of Teachers of English[1] publishes such up-to-date statements on composition as the one that follows:

QUALITIES OF EFFECTIVE WRITING PROGRAMS

Teachers and administrators involved in developing writing curricula face a complex task in reconciling public demands for educational improvement and accountability with research into the nature of composition and its effective instruction. This digest explores the components common to effective writing programs: emphasis on practice and process in writing, inservice programs, schoolwide emphasis, and administrative support.

What Are the Foundations of a Successful Writing Program?

Activities at the classroom level are the basis of any writing program. While most authorities of writing instruction agree that children learn to write by writing (Haley-James, 1981), Graves (1979) and Applebee (1981) have observed a distressing lack of classroom time devoted to extended periods of writing. At the elementary level, Graves notes that skill drills are predominant in many classrooms, and that opportunities to write complete pieces are often marred by excessive concern with mechanical "correctness." At the secondary level, Applebee reports that most writing activity is of a mechanical nature, such as "fill in the blanks" or "short answer." It is likely that any writing program will be successful only if students are given ample opportunity to perform significant writing tasks. In his description of the Vermont Writing Program, Paul Eschholz (Neill, 1982) notes that students in the program's six model schools write an average of 45 to 90 minutes *daily*.

What Elements Should Be Included in Classroom Writing Instruction?

In many programs that have grown from the Bay Area Writing Project, the emphasis is on the total process of writing, that is, on the prewriting, drafting, and revising that lead to the final product. Neill (1982) lists a core of concerns that teachers in the Bay Area Writing Project (now the National Writing Project) have cited as important to successful writing instruction: *Composing Process* (from prewriting activities through revision); *Syntax* (including sentence combining, examination of common errors, and Francis Christensen's rhetoric); *Sequence* (moving from personal to analytical writing, from thesis to logical arguments); *Small Group Technique* (peer criticism, writing for real audiences within the classroom, reading aloud in small groups); and *Writing Assessment* (holistic evaluation, systematic schoolwide assessment). The programs encourage teachers to be writers and to model writing behavior in the classroom.

In a meta-analysis of 72 experimental studies, George Hillocks (1983) found that an *environmental* mode of instruction was the most effective. In this mode, the teacher uses activities that involve high levels of student interaction, with writing activities which parallel the writing that students will encounter outside the classroom. The teachers in Applebee's 1981 study also point out that an effective writing lesson includes an active role for students, minimal teacher dominance, and natural emergence of writing out of other activities.

In summary, classroom characteristics for an effective writing program include the following:

- opportunity for students to write frequently, even in the primary grades, with delayed or "as needed" instruction in grammar;
- teachers writing with students;
- students learning to write for many audiences and in many modes, including those required in content area classrooms; and
- nonthreatening evaluation of student writing with emphasis on revision rather than correction.
(Goldberg, 1983; Graves, 1978; Howard, 1984)

How Can the Writing Teacher's Skill Be Improved?

Teachers and administrators in Neill's survey cited inservice training with periodic updates as important ingredients in successful writing programs. Inservice is most effective if it is an ongoing program rather than a "one-shot" session, and if it is on a voluntary basis. Inservice trainers should be a combination of people from inside and outside the school or the district. Neill observes that teachers have more credibility as inservice instructors than do "nonteaching experts." Enthusiasm, knowledge of current theory on the writing process, and a focus on practical application of techniques are also essential qualities for inservice trainers.

In addition, Neill's subjects advised using recognized program models with good track records. In the National Writing Project, which appears to be the most far-reaching program model, teachers attend workshops to improve their own writing skills and their teaching of writing. Participants may then act as consultants for school or district inservice sessions, so reinforcement occurs naturally. In summary, the most successful inservice programs

- are ongoing and voluntary;
- make teachers aware of the theory and research in the teaching of writing, with sessions focusing on practical applications of theory and research;
- give attention to specific skills in which teachers may be weak;
- give teachers time and opportunity to gain confidence in their ability to teach composition, allowing for structured feedback about their use of new skills;
- provide opportunities for observation in other classrooms;
- address issues that concern teachers, such as paperwork, evaluation, diagnosis, remediation, and explaining the writing program to parents; and
- involve administrators in both program and session activities.

Should Writing Instruction Be Confined to the English Classroom?

In effective writing programs, writing is viewed as an integral part of all subjects. Such a schoolwide emphasis is desirable because students will improve their understanding of the disciplines that emphasize writing, their writing ability will improve with opportunity for guided writing practice in several classrooms, students will grasp the importance of writing outside the English classroom, and effective schoolwide emphasis fosters interdepartmental cooperation (Glatthorn, 1981).

Interest in the idea of writing across the curriculum was fostered by the British Schools Council Project in Writing Across the Curriculum, which from the mid-1960s onward studied how writing (and talking) were learned and used in schools throughout the United Kingdom. James Britton and others found that in language-rich classrooms—such as science labs where teams of students freely conversed in order to solve problems raised by an experiment—transcripts of student conversations showed that the interaction sparked varied language uses, including speculation and argument, which might not have occurred in more restrained classrooms. Further research on written composition by James Britton and James Moffett found that in classrooms in which cultivation of many forms of discourse led to writing, the final products showed greater fluency and awareness of audience (Thaiss, 1983).

To orient the entire faculty to the general purposes of a curriculum-wide program, Glatthorn suggests making it clear that no blame will be placed for student writing problems. The program's emphasis will reflect teachers' needs and concerns, and will not restrict any teacher's professional autonomy in matters of student evaluation. Individual departments will determine the extent of their participation.

A curriculum-wide program can take on many forms. It can involve direct intervention by the English department in content area assignments, similar to the program at Boston University's College of Basic Studies, or it can operate informally as English teachers provide instructional materials to content area teachers, offering assistance to interested students with content area writing assignments (Lehr, 1982).

Whatever the tone or extent of the curriculum-wide emphasis, the program will best succeed when administrators

- acquire interdepartmental cooperation by ascertaining needs and perceptions of content area teachers;
- develop program objectives for both students and teachers; and
- include the elementary level, even as early as kindergarten or first grade, rather than focusing on the secondary level.

What Role Do Administrators Have in a Successful Writing Program?

Administrators at the school and district levels should make teachers aware of their strong support and commitment to writing programs. One sign of support is awareness of the status of the writing program in the school. Applebee (Neill, 1982) lists five danger signals for which principals should watch in a writing program: low or failing scores on writing tests, widespread use of objective tests, omission of writing samples from writing assessments, lack of help for students with writing problems, and complaints about declining achievement.

A second sign of commitment is support for the staff development program. Glatthorn (1981) cites studies concluding that the most successful inservice projects were jointly managed by teachers and administrators. Allowing released time or other options—such as team teaching, repeated half-day sessions so one substitute can cover the classes of two teachers, or a reduced school day—will encourage participation in inservice. Furthermore, principals and other administrators should attend and participate in training sessions to improve their own writing. Such participation also gives administrators an opportunity to evaluate the inservice meetings and to identify and reward excellent teachers as well as those striving to improve their teaching (Neill, 1982).

Finally, meeting with parents will demonstrate to the public as well as to teachers a commitment to writing improvement. Administrators can keep parents informed of student progress, suggest how they can help improve their children's writing at home, and provide assistance to parents who want to improve their own writing. Identifying and using parent talents for tutoring or inservice consulting can also be beneficial (Glatthorn, 1981).

Thus principals, superintendents, and other administrators can demonstrate essential support for writing programs by

- monitoring the writing program and the quality of its evaluation,
- actively participating in development of inservice programs,
- allowing released time or other arrangements to facilitate inservice participation,
- attending inservice sessions as participants, and
- working with parents.

Conclusion

Since components of a good writing program vary from school to school and district to district, even the finest program in the nation—if one could be identified—would not necessarily work well in a different school. However, those programs that effectively meet the instructional needs of both students and teachers as well as public demands have the above features in common. Carefully adapted to individual schools or districts, any one or all of these features can go a long way toward improving the quality of composition instruction.

Hilary Taylor Holbrook, ERIC/RCS

References

Applebee, Arthur N. *Writing in the Secondary School: English and the Content Areas*. Urbana, Ill.: National Council of Teachers of English, 1981. ED 197 347.

Glatthorn, Allan A. "Writing in the Schools: Improvement through Effective Leadership." Reston, Va.: National Association of Secondary School Principals, 1981.

Goldberg, Mark F. "Writing Objectives: The National Writing Project." *NASSP Bulletin* 67 (October 1983): 110–11.

Graves, Donald H. "Balance the Basics: Let Them Write." New York, Ford Foundation, 1978. ED 192 364.

Haley-James, Shirley M., ed. *Perspectives on Writing in Grades 1–8*. Urbana, Ill.: National Council of Teachers of English, 1981. ED 198 565.

Hillocks, George. "What Works in Teaching Composition: A Summary of Results." Paper presented at the annual convention of the National Council of Teachers of English, Denver, Colorado. November, 1983.

Howard, James. "Writing to Learn." Washington, D.C.: Council for Basic Education, 1984. ED 241 951.

Lehr, Fran. "ERIC/RCS Report: Promoting Schoolwide Writing." *English Education* 14 (February 1982): 47–52. EJ 259 357.

Neill, Shirley Bose. "Teaching Writing: Problems and Solutions. AASA Critical Issues Report." Arlington, Va.: American Association of School Administrators, 1982. ED 219 776.

Robertson, Linda R. "Stranger in a Strange Land, or Stimulating Faculty Interest in Writing Across the Curriculum." Paper presented at the annual meeting of the Wyoming Conference on Freshman and Sophomore English. Laramie, Wyoming, July, 1981. ED 211 996.

Thaiss, Christopher. "Language Across the Curriculum." Urbana, Ill. ERIC Clearinghouse on Reading and Communication Skills, 1984.

Believing that teachers hold the key to curriculum and instruction, a local Curriculum Study Commission, composed largely of practicing teachers, prepared the chart in Figure 2–1. This clear illustration of the centrality of the teacher in making curriculum decisions shows how national, state, county, and local agencies support teachers working with students at all levels of instruction.[2] This

Figure 2–1. Curriculum Governance in California

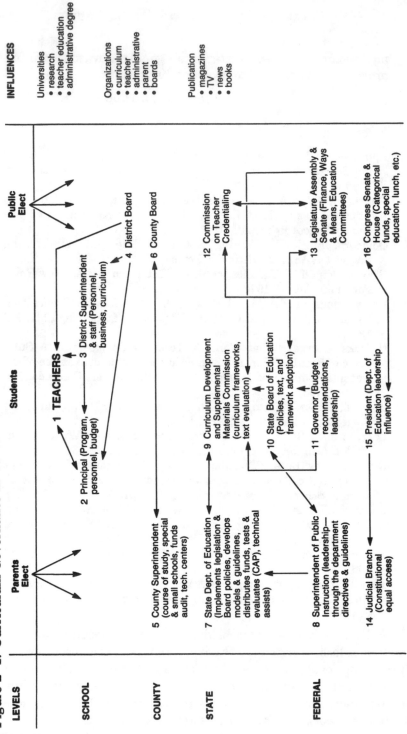

38

chart may be adapted readily to represent your state educational structure in order to show teachers clearly "where their involvement can be most productive."

You may choose to invite a consultant to work with you (someone who has particular expertise on the teaching of writing and the ability to conduct a planning workshop with teachers). This person has the advantage of recognized authority and expertise—the honor that few of us command in our home territory. You might contact the Director of the National Project site nearest you.[3]

No matter how you begin, the group of teachers will have to make the crucial decision: What do we want to do? How shall we begin? Forming three or more teams to work on specific tasks makes a huge job more manageable, for example:

Task 1:   Stating goals and objectives; a timeline

Task 2:   Compiling a list of district resources

Task 3:   Planning informational workshops in each school

Task 4:   Seeking support, funding; report to School Board

Task 5:   Outlining specific ideas for initiating the program

Task 6:   Assessing student achievement in the language arts

Task 7:   Locating exemplary programs to observe

Task 8:   Ordering or locating copies of relevant materials

After forming the task force teams, set a time for the next meeting when each group will report, adding its contribution to the information collected which will become part of a plan to present to the Superintendent and the School Board.

SUMMARY

Planning a schoolwide writing program is a worthwhile endeavor that should have long-term effects in terms of student performance as well as teacher satisfaction. It is essential that a number of teachers be involved in the planning; students, too, should be invited to have input. Every effort should be made to present writing as a means of expressing thinking about subjects taught in every classroom so that writing is not perceived as the concern only of English language arts teachers. The Writing Task Force will logically begin with an assessment of how writing is now being taught in one school or perhaps the whole district, as discussed in the next section.

How Writing Is Now Taught in Your School

We already know how writing should be taught. In the first chapter we summarized what we know about teaching writing based on current theory and practice. We know, for example, that in an effective writing program, students will:

Write frequently

Learn to write by writing

Learn to write by reading

Talk about the writing process

Write for varied purposes

Write to different audiences

See writing as a way of expressing "thinking"

Edit their own writing and that of others

Revise some writing selections to be made public

Be involved in evaluating their own progress

Confer with their instructor periodically

We now need to examine our own writing programs to determine just where they are strong and in which areas they can be improved. We need to begin asking questions, for example:

How is the writing program defined?

What are the specific goals and objectives?

Is there any evidence of a scope and sequence?

How are the individual needs of students met?

What is the role of testing in the writing program?

How are students evaluated?

What materials are being used to teach writing?

What are the quality indicators for an effective writing program?

Perhaps, most important, we need to ask: Just what are individual teachers doing in their classrooms?

An excellent checklist, "Essentials and Excellence in the English Language Arts Program," has been prepared by the California Association of Teachers of English.[4] Representing the judgment of representative teachers across the state, it identifies quality indicators that you can assess in your school for all aspects of the English language arts program, including: school, staff, curriculum, and student. The writing program involves and is affected by all of the items listed in Figure 2–2.

SUMMARY

To develop a strong writing program we need to involve in the planning those representatives from all of the component groups that are affected by the program—administrators, teachers, and students. A good writing program will be student-centered, designed to meet student needs. Instruction and materials will be selected with explicit goals in mind, for example, developing the self-esteem of each student. The writing program will begin in the English language arts classroom, but it will extend to every classroom as teachers guide students to write "thinking." Writing will also be closely connected to the reading of literature in all subject areas as students

Figure 2–2. A Position Paper of CATE—The California Association of Teachers of English

ESSENTIALS AND EXCELLENCE IN THE ENGLISH LANGUAGE ARTS PROGRAM

The following checklist, developed by the California Association of Teachers of English and representing the professional judgment of teachers from throughout the state, suggests items which identify quality programs and instruction in the English Language Arts. While student test scores or the number of days and hours in class may be easily measured, often the real indicators of the quality of a program are much more specific in a particular discipline. These guidelines may be useful both within the department as a self-evaluation instrument and for administrators and school boards who are dedicated to improving English Language Arts instruction in the schools.

I. The School and the Teaching Climate

Obviously, many of these items are appropriate to any discipline in the school program. Such things as a physically attractive classroom environment, freedom from disruption or violence, and general administrative and community support for school programs are crucial to developing an outstanding school program. But the items below are especially important to the English Language Arts program.

A. INSTRUCTIONAL MATERIALS AND EQUIPMENT

	Always	Often	Sometimes	Rarely	Never
1. Basic and supplemental texts and other materials are provided for all students.					
2. Texts and other materials are current.					
3. Texts and other instructional materials provide both variety and challenge appropriate to student grade level and ability					
4. New materials are readily available after teacher and departmental research and recommendation.					
5. Texts and materials are selected for their relationship to a carefully planned curriculum.					
6. Audio-visual equipment is accessible and maintained.					
7. Supplementary materials such as films, videotapes, audio tapes and records are available for classroom use.					
8. Computers are available where appropriate for classroom use in instruction, practice, and composing.					
9. A school library has adequate resources and acquisition policies to encourage student research and outside reading.					

B. CLASS SIZE AND TEACHING ASSIGNMENT

All learning is affected by the size of a given class, the resulting attention a teacher can give individual students, and the assignment of teachers to subject areas where they are adequately prepared. Moreover, all teachers function more effectively when their daily work is not cluttered by out-of-class reports, unnecessary paperwork, and additional supervision assignments which take time away from classroom preparation, and when they sense that non-classroom assignments are distributed equally among teachers. However, the fact that students require sufficient reading and writing skills to function in any academic course suggests that these items are especially important in identifying quality English Language Arts programs. The National Council of Teachers of English recommends that, ideally, English teachers teach no more than 100 students per day in four classes because of the time required to attend to student essays in a meaningful way.

	Always	Often	Sometimes	Rarely	Never
1. Classes which include a significant component in the teaching of writing number 20 to 25 students.					
2. The teacher's school day includes specified times for preparation, planning, sharing with colleagues, and evaluation of student work.					
3. The teacher's academic preparation, strengths, and interests are incorporated into assignment to particular courses.					
4. The number of different classroom preparations is limited to two or three.					
5. Time is provided during the school day, other than in the teacher's preparation period, for student/teacher conferences about essays or other work.					
6. All teachers of English Language Arts classes have preparation in both the content and the methods of teaching English Language Arts.					

43

C SCHOOL AND ADMINISTRATIVE SUPPORT

Teachers in all disciplines can do a better job of teaching if their surroundings are conducive to good teaching; for example, they have adequate office or classroom space for student conferences, for preparation, and for storage and filing of materials. Also central to a good teaching climate are administrative support in such matters as reducing classroom interruptions; developing public support and awareness through recognition of teacher and student achievement; and developing awareness of teacher workload and working conditions. In addition, these items create a climate which fosters excellence in the teaching of the English Language Arts.

	Always	Often	Sometimes	Rarely	Never
1. School administrators acknowledge the importance of sound English Language Arts instruction to the total school program and demonstrate that support in administrative decisions about class size, budget, assignment of non-classroom duties, and other areas.					
2. Teachers in all academic departments have a commitment to reinforce principles and practices consistent with good reading and writing instruction.					
3. Counselors work with the English Department for appropriate placement of students in English classes.					
4. Student and teacher achievements in writing or other English Language Arts activities are publicized in the school and in the local press.					
5. Administrators and teachers in other academic disciplines foster a positive attitude about the importance of effective written and oral communication, both by models of good use of the language and by classroom practice.					
6. In such ways as providing reading time or writing time during the school day, the school program encourages students to take time for recreational reading and personal writing.					
7. Administrators visit English Language Arts classes, perhaps teach them occasionally, and provide time for inter-disciplinary exchanges of classroom visits among teachers.					

44

II. Staff Preparation

Because competence in the English Language Arts is so essential to successful student performance in all academic areas and activities, the preparation and placement of highly trained personnel in English classes are crucial to the success of the entire school program; however, staff members untrained in the content and methods of English Language Arts are frequently assigned to English classes simply because it is assumed that any educated person can teach English. Moreover, the quality of teaching and adequate preparation of staff are closely tied to such non-academic factors as adequate entry-level salaries, provision of sabbatical and leave time and released time for conferences, workshops, or research, and transfer credit for previous teaching experience. Outstanding programs in English depend on quality preparation of staff in both academic and on-going programs.

A. PROFESSIONAL BACKGROUND AND TRAINING

	Always	Often	Sometimes	Rarely	Never
1. English Language Arts teachers have academic preparation in composition, literature, oral language, and related subjects studied by English majors and minors.					
2. English Language Arts teachers have training in the content and methods of English Language Arts instruction.					
3. New teachers receive adequate support with teaching ideas and materials from experienced teachers and administrators.					

B. PROFESSIONAL DEVELOPMENT

	Always	Often	Sometimes	Rarely	Never
1. Members of the English Language Arts staff are active in professional organizations through attendance at conferences, workshops, and related professional activities.					
2. Released time and financial assistance are available for continuing professional development activities on a regular basis.					
3. Inservice education programs are designed for and by English Language Arts teachers to meet the needs of staff and students.					
4. Opportunities and released time exist for staff participation in demonstration teaching, peer visits, and departmental sharing of ideas and methods in order to develop and improve teaching skills.					
5. A mentor teacher is available with help and released time to develop ideas, teaching strategies, and curriculum.					
6. Department files of materials and teaching ideas are maintained and updated for new and experienced personnel.					
7. A school or departmental library of supplementary and professional materials is available, and acquisitions are frequently updated.					

III. Curriculum

The coordinated curriculum for an effective English Language Arts program grows from a statement of philosophy which focuses on the interrelatedness at all grade levels of the language processes of reading, writing, speaking, listening, and thinking, and includes a planned curriculum for the content areas of oral language and communication, reading and literature, writing and composition, and development of form in grammar, mechanics, spelling and penmanship.

A. GENERAL

While it is important for any good school program to have clearly stated goals and a coherent, well-planned curriculum, it is perhaps most important to consider the development and articulation of English Language Arts programs across disciplines, grades, and schools. Because the discipline is so diverse, the English Language Arts can become fragmented into incomplete components reducible to test-measurable items without attention to such issues as those listed below. The strong English Language Arts program offers a rigorous academic content for all students, emphasizes a balance of all the language arts skills and provides for a continuous monitoring of students' progress and regular evaluation of the program itself.

	Always	Often	Sometimes	Rarely	Never
1. The curriculum grows from a coherent statement of philosophy developed and supported by the English Language Arts staff, which also participates in the development of language arts philosophies and programs at the district level.					
2. The English Language Arts curriculum is articulated with that of other programs in the district to provide a clear, logical sequence of Language Arts skills, activities, and growth through the elementary, middle, and high school levels.					
3. The English Language Arts curriculum, by providing a variety of literature, writing, and speaking activities, addresses the needs and growth of a wide range of students, remedial through advanced, minority and second-language, and the physically and educationally disabled.					
4. The English Language Arts curriculum is based upon current research and practice in the elements of reading, writing, speaking, and listening as they relate to language acquisition and growth.					
5. The English Language Arts curriculum is regularly reviewed and revised, according to changes in student needs, teacher perceptions, and current research.					
6. The English Language Arts staff is open to the need for innovation and participation in the regular review, change, and updating of the curriculum.					

	Always	Often	Sometimes	Rarely	Never

B. ARTICULATION

1. The English Language Arts curriculum provides an appropriate continuum of language arts activities and skills, articulated among the elementary, middle, and high school levels, to avoid repetition and duplication.

2. The English Language Arts program is supported by reading and writing practices within other academic disciplines in the school and includes appropriate reading materials and writing activities from other disciplines.

3. The English Language Arts staff meets regularly as a department and with teachers from other schools in the district to explore and resolve curriculum issues of common interest.

4. The English Language Arts program attends to particular local needs of students and the community and to important principles, research, and practices characteristic of the Language Arts discipline.

5. The English Language Arts program facilitates the transition of students from minority language programs into programs of English language fluency.

6. The English Language Arts staff communicates frequently about students and programs with staff members responsible for students with language handicaps, second-language limitations, and other types of language-related problems.

7. The district's curriculum guidelines and such models as the State Department of Education's *Model Curriculum Standards, Reading/Language Arts Framework,* and handbooks for Literature, Writing, and Oral Language are consulted in the development of curriculum materials which also incorporate attention to local needs.

C. ORAL LANGUAGE AND COMMUNICATION

1. Student development of oral language is a focus of the English Language Arts program at all grades and ability levels.

2. Students participate in organized activities requiring oral expression, such as discussions, reports, interviews, and play-reading and performance.

3. Students have opportunities to develop attentive listening skills and to relate information acquired by active listening.

4. A curriculum exists to facilitate the transition of students in minority-language programs to programs of language fluency.

	Always	Often	Sometimes	Rarely	Never

D. READING AND LITERATURE

1. All students have the opportunity to study in depth a core of district- and department-selected works of literary merit.

2. Reading and literature are taught and studied as related subjects and connected with writing, speaking, and listening activities in an integrated English Language Arts program.

3. Students and teachers read and discuss good books for both instruction and recreation.

4. Instruction in reading and literature enables students to read on several levels of understanding, including the literal, interpretive, applicative, analytical, and critical.

5. A range of reading selections provides material appropriate for study at a variety of student ability and interest levels.

6. Students read, discuss, and respond to a balanced, broad spectrum of literary works, e.g., those by American and European authors, male and female authors, and minority authors; and works representing a variety of cultures.

7. Students read, discuss, and respond to a variety of important themes in a range of genres, including novels, short stories, plays, essays, poetry, and non-fiction.

	Always	Often	Sometimes	Rarely	Never

E. WRITING AND COMPOSITION

1. A coherent, schoolwide writing program exists, such as those models outlined by the California Writing Project or by the State Department of Education's *Model Curriculum Standards* and the *Handbook for Planning an Effective Writing Program.*

2. Writing and composition are taught as part of an integrated Language Arts program, not in isolation.

3. The writing program develops in students the skills, confidence, and fluency to handle competently a variety of writing tasks in any academic discipline or job.

4. Students have the opportunity to write for a variety of purposes, such as to explore thinking, to learn, to express their feelings, and to respond or analyze.

5. Students have opportunities to write in a variety of modes, for a range of audiences, in a range of styles and voices: descriptive and narrative, persuasive and expository, formal and informal, creative and critical.

6. Students have frequent practice in the various stages of the development of a piece of writing, from pre-writing, through drafting, responding, and revising, to evaluation and publication.

7. Students develop their skills at revision, response, and evaluation through use of peer response groups to discuss their writing.

8. Writing activities and composition assignments help develop higher order thinking skills such as critical thinking and reading, logic, and argument.

9. Students who have developed fluency and confidence with writing learn to attend to form and conventions, such as spelling, grammar, and mechanics.

10. Students have a variety of opportunities for informal and formal evaluation and response to their writing from peers and teacher.

11. Students are motivated to write voluntarily for personal reflection and expression.

IV. The Students and the Community

The outcome of any outstanding English program must be to produce a literate, thinking society, while the goal of any significant school must be to develop the highest expectations for all its students. More immediately, a strong English Language Arts program has specific goals for its students and the community at large.

A. THE STUDENTS

	Always	Often	Sometimes	Rarely	Never
1. Student growth in English Language Arts skills and competence is measured by students' confidence in approaching new language-related situations rather than solely by improvements in test scores.					
2. Students leave with both a depth of study in literature, language, and composition, and a breadth of language arts experiences.					
3. Students leave the program with an interest in recreational reading and personal writing, and with an enthusiasm for further study in language arts subjects.					
4. Students are willing to approach peers or teacher for help with reading and writing activities.					
5. Students participate actively and enthusiastically, both in and out of class, in the language-related activities of reading, writing, and discussion.					
6. Students participate in the development of reading and writing goals for themselves and feel they can achieve the high goals outlined by the teacher for their reading and writing development.					
7. Students' interest and achievement in English Language Arts programs are manifested in their participation in such language-related programs as journalism courses, drama courses, newspaper and literary magazine production, plays, debates, and contests.					

B. THE COMMUNITY

	Always	Often	Sometimes	Rarely	Never
1. The community widely rewards and recognizes student achievement in the English Language Arts.					
2. Parents provide models demonstrating the importance of the English Language Arts by their own reading, writing, and discussion.					
3. Parents talk with students about the books students are reading, the papers they are writing, and English assignments they are completing.					
4. English Language Arts activities and assignments receive positive emphasis and time commitments in the home.					
5. Parents provide support for student development of language arts skills and growth without interfering with the student's growth or superimposing their own knowledge and style on the child's exploration of his or her language.					
6. Teachers clearly communicate expectations about curriculum and behavior to students and parents.					
7. Teachers communicate with parents about positive achievements in English Language Arts classes in addition to communicating about students' language arts problems.					
8. Parents provide a suitable atmosphere and time for students to complete reading and writing assignments.					

learn to write like a scientist and to use writing as a way of clarifying their thinking.

The Students You Teach

Students learn what we teach them, as expressed in the following anonymous poem:

Children Learn What They Live

If a child lives with criticism,
    He learns to condemn.
If a child lives with hostility,
    He learns to fight.
If a child lives with ridicule,
    He learns to be shy.
If a child lives with tolerance,
    He learns to be patient.
If a child lives with encouragement,
    He learns confidence.
If a child lives with praise,
    He learns to appreciate.
If a child lives with fairness,
    He learns justice.
If a child lives with security,
    He learns to have faith.
If a child lives with approval,
    He learns to like himself.
If a child lives with acceptance and friendship,
    He learns to find love in the world.

To be effective, a writing program must be student-centered in every respect—curriculum, methodology, and evaluation.[5] Therefore, we need to think carefully about the students in each classroom of the district. We must be aware of the latest research about learning styles, multicultural education, English as a second language, and so on. We want to share ideas that will engage students in writing "thinking" and in communicating with each other. Above all, we want to involve students in making decisions that affect them. Even young students can discuss problems and suggest fair solutions. We need to permit the learners themselves to participate in curriculum development and plans for evaluation of the writing program as well as the evaluation of student achievement.

STUDENT INVOLVEMENT IN PLANNING

Students should be involved in curriculum planning from the very beginning. As you develop a writing program, it is important that representative students sit on committees and serve actively in presenting ideas to the School Board. Students can conduct discussions with other students in classrooms to generate suggestions for program development that may prove enlightening and innovative.

Students should also have input into decisions regarding evaluation of student performance in writing. Recognizing that evaluation is *for* students as well as teachers, administrators, and parents, we need to consider the kinds of evaluation that really communicate progress. Techniques such as the following will serve this purpose.

1. The Writing Portfolio: Here is a clear picture of what a student has accomplished over a given period of time. Its chronological arrangement will show progress.

2. Learning Logs: Individual logs kept during a unit of study or in response to reading a book reveal a student's learning and his or her active participation with thinking processes expressed through writing.

3. Individual Contracts: The student selects the specific activities, establishes a reasonable timeline, and evaluates his or her own progress at specified checkpoints.

4. Student-Teacher Conferences: Each individual student meets with the teacher to discuss current work, progress over several weeks, and plans for future development. The student prepares for the conference by making a self-assessment to share with the instructor who responds with

comments based on his or her perception of the student's achievement and needs for further development.

Let students talk about their perception of evaluation. They should have an input into decisions that affect their learning and their sense of self-worth.

STUDENT-CENTERED INSTRUCTION

Instructional strategies should also be selected with student needs in mind. For example, students respond to positive models for any activity—football, drama, teaching, writing, and the like. Few students, however, see adults who model writing as a positive, challenging activity. For this reason, we may plan to bring writers to the schools to talk about their work, their compulsion to write, how they work, and so on. Most authors who write for young people are excited about writing and about their audience. The teacher can also serve as a model who sees writing as important. Teachers should write with their students and share the results, even the problems they have getting started or staying with the task. Modeling is an effective teaching strategy.

Students may also be inspired by what "real" writers say about their work. Quotations about writing displayed in the room may provide the stimulus for talking about writing. Begin collecting a variety, for example:

"The desire for writing grows with writing."
                                        Erasmus

"The difference between the right word and the almost right word is the difference between lightning and the lightning bug."
                                        Mark Twain

"True ease in writing comes from art, not chance."
                                        Alexander Pope

"Draw your chair up close to the edge of the precipice and I'll tell you a story."
                                        F. Scott Fitzgerald

"Reading is seeing by proxy."
        Herbert Spencer

"Meaning is a form of negotiation in language."
        Jerome Bruner

"The mind is a muscle, and a muscle not used will atrophy."
        Susan Sontag

"This is my letter to the world
that never wrote to me."
        Emily Dickinson

"I celebrate myself and sing myself."
        Walt Whitman

Pictures of writers also serve to make authors real. Featuring pictures of such poets as e. e. cummings, William Penn Warren, and Robert Frost will help boys realize that men write poetry as well as prose.

Perhaps the most important consideration is our own attitude toward students. Can we project a genuine liking for the young people who come into our classrooms? Do we feel real enthusiasm and respect for students' ideas? "The teacher-student relationship is at the heart of the educational experience."[6]

APPROPRIATE EXPECTATIONS

Our overall goal for curriculum development is to nurture each student's growth to his or her fullest potential. Thus, as we plan objectives for a writing program, we need to keep constantly in mind the individuality of the students with whom we work, the differences in their intellectual abilities, and their experiential backgrounds. Our expectations must be realistic.

Yet, our expectations can motivate students to perform amazingly well. Studies show that students will perform for teachers who expect them to achieve. Reported under the title, *Pygmalion in the Classroom*, Rosenthal and Jacobson's study suggests possible effects of teacher expectations on students whom the teacher expects to succeed.[7]

Conversely, Shipman's study found that children from low-income families entered school with high degrees of self-esteem, but dropped in their self-esteem compared to middle-class children after three years in school.[8] As teachers, we need to plan for developing self-esteem in all students, and writing can provide an important opportunity.

TALKING WITH YOUNG WRITERS

Talk with students about improving their writing. Even the youngest students will have ideas that they can compile on an inspirational poster to be displayed. Shown here is an example of a poster prepared by a group of ninth graders.

How to Improve Your Writing
1. Read the work of good writers.
2. Write about what you know.
3. Think a lot about what you plan to write.
4. Write every day.
5. Read what you have written aloud.
6. Keep a Writing Folder or Notebook.
7. Ask other people to read your writing.
8. Expand your vocabulary.
9. Jot down ideas as you think of them.
10. Refer to books about writing for help.

These students are involved in writing. A workshop attitude permeates the room as each person, including the teacher, works on his or her writing. They frequently share examples of good writing in fiction and nonfiction they are reading, perhaps a newspaper column such as Ellen Goodman's extended metaphor that compares the rescue of Humphrey, a whale that lost its way in San Francisco Bay, to our country's Latin American policy. After discussing the writer's need to perceive events and objects in different, more creative ways, the students generate other metaphors that might be developed following Goodman's model. Motivation is not a problem for these young writers.

SUMMARY

As we plan a writing program, we need to consider the students we teach. Student-centered instruction is positive and realistic. It is presented by a teacher who clearly cares about student needs and establishes achievement goals that are appropriate for the age and ability levels of his or her students. Workshop approaches support student self-esteem and encourage all students to grow to their fullest potential.

Model for a Holistic, Student-Centered Program

The holistic model presented in Figure 2–3 is an attempt to involve students in writing as they record thoughts, express ideas, and share awareness. It is based on a strong oral language foundation and relies heavily on the support of reading. It does not, on the other hand, ignore syntax, spelling, and other conventions used by the writer, but teaches such concepts as needed in the context of the writing process.

DEFINING THIS HOLISTIC APPROACH

The term *holistic* is derived from the same Greek root as our word *whole*. The holistic model described here approaches writing as a total language act, involving thinking, listening, speaking, and reading. Because you begin building a strong support system before the students put words on paper, teaching writing as part of the whole languaging process guarantees success for each student from the beginning of the program.

The holistic model focuses first on students' *oral language facility*, because students cannot learn to write or read until they have a reasonable command of the language they are to use. Focusing on oral language emphasizes the crucial nature of language experiences during the preschool years, for if the home has not provided a rich linguistic environment, the school must provide enrichment

Figure 2–3. Focusing on Composition: Framework for a Language Arts Curriculum

Source: Tiedt/Bruemmer/Lane/Stelwagon/Watanabe/Williams, *Teaching Writing in K–8 Classrooms: The Time Has Come,* © 1983 Prentice Hall, p. 8. Reprinted by permission of Prentice Hall, Inc., Englewood Cliffs, New Jersey.

as soon as possible. Therefore, oral language development should be the primary consideration of junior and senior high school teachers working with students who are not successful writers and readers. Oral language should be emphasized as a way of learning from primary grades on.

Be aware that this model is equally applicable at any instructional level. Whenever we begin working with a new group of students, we need to assess their oral language abilities and to offer opportunities for developing oral language skills. Furthermore, the oral language foundation remains an important supportive element throughout the writing curriculum.

The second stage in the writing program, *writing fluency,* emerges naturally out of oral language experiences as students

write lists of words on a theme, compose "Fortunately/Unfortu-
nately" stories, or copy the lyrics of their favorite song. Journal
writing is an excellent writing activity at this time. The *finger exercises* used at this point must be short, and they must be activities
at which all students can succeed easily. Ideas produced during these
fluency activities are shared within the classroom, but they are not
graded. The aim of instruction at this beginning stage is to create
a positive, "I can" attitude toward writing and to assist students in
increasing the quantity that they are able and willing to write.

As students begin producing writing successfully, the *telling
of stories*, first orally, provides a stimulating focus for engaging students in writing. At this stage, reading can support writing effectively as students observe the writer's way of presenting a narrative.
After reading a story aloud, we can discuss content, organization,
and character development, which are the aspects of writing that
students should remember as they compose original stories. You
might choose stories that will lead to student writing of short mem-
oirs or personal narratives and stories that evoke memories of childhood, for example, "First Confession" by Frank O'Connor or
"Charles" by Shirley Jackson. With elementary students you might
read *Stevie* by John Steptoe or *Confessions of an Only Child* by
Norma Klein. Talk about how these authors handle dialogue, perhaps duplicating a page from the story that the students can examine to observe the use of indentation, quotation marks, dialect,
and varied synonyms for *said*. Above all, we want to present these
authors as real people who write with pencil, pen, typewriter, or
computer, much as the students do themselves.

Writing nonfiction should be introduced in the same way by
sharing examples of excellent writing—biography, essay, letter, article, and so on. Although many elements usually associated with
narrative writing also appear in nonfiction, point out some of the
differences such as the logically developed paragraph that argues
or expounds. You may teach students a formula paragraph (1 paragraph = 1 topic sentence + 3 supporting sentences + 1 concluding
sentence) as a scaffolding device, but make it clear that this is not
real writing. Encourage them to add creative imagery and to consider aspects of style appropriate for expository prose. Point out that
some of the best writing done today is nonfiction in such publications
as *The New Yorker* or collections of essays by such writers as Lewis

Thomas and James Baldwin. Macrorie's "I-Search" paper (described on page 79) is recommended for involving students in purposeful research reporting.

After students are involved in expressing their ideas in writing and are producing fluent writing, they will be motivated to examine their own *sentences* to see how they can be improved. Take this opportunity to focus on style, to discuss grammatical concepts, to introduce parallelism, or to guide students to observe the importance of sentence variety. Have students examine the sentences of the authors whose writing they are reading as they experiment with borrowed sentences, writing in the manner of Ernest Hemmingway or Judy Blume. Discuss the expanding of sentences to include more detail as well as the combining of sentences to achieve the desired flow of language.

Next, we focus on *words*, which brings in the study of word choice and usage. Students can study the fine art of choosing the most effective words as they consider connotations as well as denotations of words. (This is a good time to introduce the Mark Twain quotation on page 54.) Students can have fun playing with words— palindromes, euphemisms, conundrums—and they can extend their vocabularies as they use the dictionary and the thesaurus. A natural interest in the spellings of words borrowed from other languages and the origin of some of the strange characteristics of American spelling may lead to a fascinating language study. Students might discuss the sociolinguistic aspects of knowing how to spell.

The focus on *editing* has been placed toward the top of this triangular model because students need both experience with writing and specific instruction before they are prepared to handle this task well. At the same time, however, the simple editing technique of reading sentences aloud is introduced in the very first stages of writing. We teach students to check the grammaticality of what they write by testing the words against their "ear for language," asking themselves, "Does it sound right?" This linguistically sound method works well for native speakers of a language.

Students who have observed the punctuation of dialogue, have noted the conventions of capitalizing titles, and are aware of some odd English spellings may use proofreader's marks when editing each other's writing to note changes that should be made in re-writing the *manuscript*. As students become involved in writing, they will be motivated to edit for content, clarity, and logical development, helping each other to improve their writing. As they edit, of course, they are also dealing with evaluation, observing what makes some writing more effective than others. This is cooperative learning at its best.

Both editing and *rewriting* should be done for a specific purpose. Students who write every day will be producing many first drafts; not all are worth revising. Provide opportunities for classroom publications that give students a reason for revising selected work. Encourage them to work in pairs or small groups as they contribute to the development of each other's ideas. Publication may take the form of display on the bulletin board, a story to share with parents, duplicated pages stapled together to form an informal collection of student writing on a given topic, or an offset production with an attractively designed cover.

Following this model provides a framework for writing programs in first grade to twelfth grade. The model can be covered in ten weeks or thirty. It offers a viable sequence that involves students in writing that potentially covers all genres and can incorporate instruction on all aspects of writing. The model also leaves space for you to insert all of your favorite writing lessons so they become part of a planned scope and sequence.

ASSUMPTIONS AND IMPLICATIONS

A number of basic assumptions underlie this holistic model for writing instruction. Identifying these assumptions may enable us to discuss the implications for instruction that are implicit.

Students learn to write by writing.

Students need to write frequently, and it is recognized that teachers cannot "correct" or even read everything their students will write. Alternative and more effective ways of editing and evaluating student writing, such as peer editing, should be used.

Students need to develop oral language fluency before they can be expected to write.

Oral language activities such as reading aloud by teachers should be considered an integral part of the reading/writing program. Writing activities should always be preceded by oral warm-up discussions, and students may be taught to "speak-a-sentence" before writing it.

Students need to feel successful if they are to continue trying to write.

Positive evaluation must be provided to encourage student efforts. Teachers should consciously remove as many obstacles as possible so that students can succeed. For example, writing words on a given theme on the board during a brainstorming session (prewriting) suggests content to write about and also provides assistance with spelling key vocabulary.

Writing is an individualized process.

Students working on the same activity will achieve according to their individual abilities. Their success should be measured according to these same abilities.

Writing cannot be taught in isolation.

Writing is supported by prewriting listening, speaking, and reading activities that feed the brain and trigger thinking. Writing must be taught in an integrated language arts program that engages the student in coordinating both right and left brain abilities.

Students need to write for audiences other than their teachers.

As part of the writing lesson, teachers should schedule time for the students to share with one another in small groups. Such approaches facilitate editing and remove the teacher from the exclusively evaluative role. Peer evaluation is a stronger motivation to students to improve writing than simply writing for the teacher.

Students learn grammar intuitively, beginning with the acquisition of language in preschool years.

Students will continue to develop an "ear for language" as they listen to mature speakers and read the writing of skilled authors, for grammar is not learned by memorizing rules for producing grammatical sentences, but rather by generalizing from the language in our environments. Therefore, teachers should strive to provide a rich linguistic environment from which each student can develop an accurate ear for how English is used so that students can then test the grammaticality of their own sentences against the knowledge they have acquired.

Evaluation and grading are not synonymous terms as applied to student writing.

Grading implies comparing or ranking a student's writing against that of others in a group, often measured against a scale or set of criteria that may not be explicit. *Evaluation* seems to be a broader, less negative term, meaning to appraise, to determine the value of a piece of writing. Surely every piece of student writing has some value that we can point out to the young writer while at the same time we can suggest ways of increasing the value of his or her efforts. Self-esteem will be enhanced as students begin to learn to value their own writing and that of others in their classrooms.

SUMMARY

The writing process is a continuum that begins in the preschool years and continues into adulthood. Therefore, we should not expect young writers to produce publishable first drafts. Rather, we should make it possible for students to enjoy writing in order to ensure that they will continue to write and to grow in their ability to write effectively. The holistic model for a writing curriculum presented here provides a framework that you can implement at all levels of instruction with students who have varied abilities. It is designed to begin with the individual's own language, with the student involved in communicating experiences that are familiar, and to move upward and outward as the students gain confidence in the acceptability of what they have to say.

Reflection

A strong writing program is part of a well-conceived English language arts curriculum that builds on the resources offered by the home, community, school, and nation. Although the teacher is the key to implementing a strong English language arts program that emphasizes writing "thinking," the curriculum must be designed to meet the needs of students, and students should rightfully be included in curriculum development. Inherent in planning the goals and objectives for the English program and the instructional strategies that will be used to carry it out are plans for evaluation. Here, too, students should be involved as well as teachers. Thus, an ideal English language arts program will feature frequent writing through integrative activities and the program will be student-centered.

Challenge

The following activities provide avenues for getting started with plans for developing the writing program throughout your school district.

1. Replicate the chart presented on page 38 with appropriate changes to fit your state and county structures. Make the chart large enough to present to the School Board or a group of teachers with whom you want to discuss curriculum development.

2. Announce a meeting focusing on "Student Writing" in your school or district. Invite students and teachers to attend the meeting to brainstorm ways of improving writing instruction. Select several recommendations to implement as soon as feasible.

3. Plan a study to determine exemplary practices in teaching writing in your district. Hold a mini-conference at which teachers can present their teaching strategies.

Endnotes

1. Reprinted by permission of the National Council of Teachers of English, 1111 Kenyon Rd., Urbana, IL 61801.

2. Additional copies of this document may be obtained from the Curriculum Study Commission, 1364 Grizzly Peak Blvd., Berkeley, CA 94708.

3. For information about the National Writing Project, call 415/642-0963, or write to the National Writing Project, University of California, Tolman Hall, Berkeley, CA 94729.

4. This document is from the California Association of Teachers of English, Box 4427, Whittier, CA 90607. February 1986.

5. James Moffett and Betty Jane Wagner. *The Student-Centered Language Arts and Reading Curriculum, K–13*, 2nd ed. Boston: Houghton-Mifflin, 1983.

6. California State Department of Education. *Model Curriculum Standards, 9–12*. 1985, p. E-2.

7. Robert Rosenthal and Lenore Jacobson. *Pygmalion in the Classroom*. New York: Holt, 1968.

8. Virginia Shipman et al. *Young Children and Their First School Experiences*. Educational Testing Service, 1976.

Exploring Further

In addition to the material listed under Endnotes, the following books will suggest additional ideas for improving your writing program and will provide valuable background information for teachers of composition.

California State Department of Education. *Model Curriculum Standards, Grades Nine through Twelve*. Sacramento, 1985.

California State Department of Education. *Handbook for Planning an Effective Writing Program*, 3rd ed. Sacramento, 1986.

Foster, David. *Primer for Writing Teachers: Theories, Theorists, Issues, Problems*. Boynton/Cook, 1983.

Gere, Anne R., ed. *Roots in the Sawdust: Writing to Learn across the Disciplines*. National Council of Teachers of English, 1985.

Graves, Donald. *Writing: Teachers and Children at Work*. Heinemann, 1982.

Mohr, Marian. *Revision: The Rhythm of Meaning*. Boynton/Cook, 1984.

Shaughnessy, Mina. *Errors and Expectations*. Oxford, 1977.

Taba, Hilda. *Curriculum Development: Theory and Practice*. Harcourt, 1962.

Tiedt, Iris M. *The Language Arts Handbook*. Prentice-Hall, 1983.

Tiedt, Iris M. et al. *Teaching Writing in K–8 Classrooms*. Prentice-Hall, 1983.

3

Teaching Beginning Evaluation and Editing Skills

I can't write five words but I change seven.

Dorothy Parker

You and your students will benefit equally if you teach them how to begin evaluating and editing their own writing. As students become involved in these tasks, you will gradually feel that dreaded paperload easing off your shoulders. Also, your students will learn more about writing through these learning experiences than through your "correcting" errors they make. Our instructional goal will move from error avoidance to communicating thinking effectively. Writing will become an enjoyable learning activity as students express and share their ideas.

Naturally, students do not learn how to evaluate and edit their writing effectively overnight. Therefore, we present an approach that moves gradually toward greater independence in editing. As students assume responsibility for their own work, they also take greater pride in their accomplishments.

After reading this chapter, you should be able to:

1. Build students' oral foundation for writing

2. Talk with students about the qualities of good writing

3. Begin an editing program with your students

4. Assume the role of colleague in a writing workshop

5. Plan instruction focusing on specific aspects of writing

The Teacher's Role

Teachers work too hard when it comes to correcting students' writing, and the sad thing is that all this effort does not teach students how to write. "Bleeding" all over a student's writing has only negative effects. By teaching your students how to evaluate, edit, and revise their own writing, they will gradually learn to think and to communicate their thinking through writing. They will learn to identify the qualities of good writing and they will enjoy experimenting with interesting stylistic devices, varied grammatical structures, and different forms of writing.

TALKING ABOUT WRITING

Talk with students about writing. Discuss such ideas as the following:

1. What you write in the classroom is a first draft. No one expects your first draft to be perfect. It is not ready to be made public (to be published).

2. All published writers rework their writing many times. (See the Dorothy Parker quote at the beginning of the chapter.) Poetry especially requires much reworking because of the limited number of words used. (Model your own writing efforts for students.)

3. Editing is more than just correcting surface features such as punctuation and spelling. It means rereading lines and pages. It means changing phrases and sentences or even throwing away a whole page that simply does not fit. The writer is always trying to improve his or her writing by

choosing the most effective words, making the sentences flow, and developing intriguing images.

4. Everything that you write will not be of equal value. You will revise or polish only selected pieces of writing that are really worth spending time on. You may choose to edit something that especially interests you or a piece of writing that has an important purpose, for example, a letter to an editor.

As a teacher, you can provide purposes for writing so that students have reasons for revising their work. Initiate class or school publications as an outlet for student writing. Encourage students to become involved in local or national issues that may lead to the writing of articles for the local newspaper or letters to government officials in an attempt to effect change. Of course, one purpose can be to learn how to write more effectively, and students with whom you have developed rapport will respond to that reason for polishing their work as they begin to see themselves as "writers" who have something to say. Providing real purpose for writing makes school work have an immediacy that is exciting and motivating.

DEVELOPING A WORKSHOP ATMOSPHERE

An important aspect of the writing program is the classroom climate. Do students sense immediately that they as individuals are acceptable to the teacher? Is there warmth? a smile? Do they soon recognize the expectation that they will write *together* every day, that not only will they learn how to write more effectively but that the process will be enjoyable? The following suggestions will help you make it clear that you operate a student-centered classroom.

Treat your students like "real writers" who have enrolled in a writers' workshop.

Clearly defining your expectations and attitudes will have great influence on student performance. Try to serve the role of facilitator—a person who picks up on student concerns or provides the liaison with the school administration in order to enable students to get things done. Work *with* your students rather than dominating the classroom as the person for whom the students write with the sole purpose of "getting a good grade." Students who really become involved in writing will accept responsibility for improving their own writing and will be self-motivated. They will then write because *they want to write!*

Write with your students.

Share yourself as you also compose a memory story or write in your Reading Log. This process will be enlightening as you try to do what you ask students to do. Join the student writer groups to read your writing and to share your problems in developing a piece of writing. Thus, you model the writing process—a process that students do not often observe adults engaged in. In this writing workshop, you, too, are a learner as you try to improve your writing and experience the same problems the students do.

Let students discover how to write.

The secure teacher does not need to tell students everything in order to maintain a role of authority. Share the excitement of student learning as they discover how Mark Twain writes dialogue or how John Updike describes Holden Caulfield. Students can literally discover everything they need to know about writing from the literature they read and from each other. Your role will be to serve as the guide on this Great Expedition.

Let's step down from the podium from which we lecture, telling students all they ought to know and then testing them on how much they can remember. True reform in education demands that we retrain ourselves and our students to engage actively in learning, to work for the thrill of discovering new knowledge, and to value intrinsic rewards rather than teacher-given grades. Such strategies as cooperative learning, peer tutoring, small-group responses to work in progress, and self-evaluation make teaching easier, more stimulating, and more rewarding.

SUMMARY

Teachers need to understand new ways of working with the writing process that will not only be more effective with students but will also make the instructional task easier. Teachers must learn to play a facilitative role as they support what students are trying to do. We know now that teachers should not be copy editors for students nor should teachers expect even to read everything their students write. With this paperload lifted from their shoulders, teachers can work with their students to discover ideas and to begin expressing these ideas powerfully and creatively.

Developing an "Ear for Language"

The ability to evaluate and edit anyone's writing depends on the reader's knowledge of language. We judge a sentence to be fluent or gramatically acceptable based on our experience with the English language. We acquire this knowledge of language through hearing English spoken and through reading it over the years. We constantly test language that we hear or read against our knowledge of English grammar and idiom. We continue to develop this "ear for language" as we receive additional linguistic input.

Be aware that the students you work with are adding daily to their knowledge of language. Therefore, as part of our writing program, we deliberately plan classroom activities that add to students' oral-aural facility with language to build a foundation for working with written language. We can also help them become aware of this learning process and how it affects their writing.

Instructional strategies that add to student knowledge of language are those that also stimulate listening and speaking. The same strategies will promote and enable students to gain power over writing and reading. We will discuss the following methods of developing this vital "ear for language" that is necessary for editing:

Reading Writing Aloud

Talking in Small Groups about Ideas

Identifying What Students Know about Language

READING WRITING ALOUD

With the current emphasis on teaching literature at all levels and developing a literature-based language arts/reading program in the elementary school, all of us should consider how we can engage students with literature more effectively. Begin by presenting literature as writing done by another human being with whom students can enter into a transaction. Reading literature selections aloud is an excellent method for assuring that all students, especially those "at risk," have an opportunity to know good literature.

Reading writing aloud to students is the most effective strategy we can use to expose them to skillful writing. By doing so, we enable them to continue language acquisition as they begin to learn the standard dialect that we want them to write. At all ages, students learn readily through hearing; thus, reading aloud to them each day extends their knowledge of English and just how good writers use it to achieve their purposes.

Reading aloud should never be considered as an extra, something you use as a reward or a time filler. Reading all kinds of literature (writing) aloud should be part of your daily lesson plans in any classroom, for this strategy serves to teach many skills and concepts. As you read *Charlotte's Web* or *The Good Earth* aloud, students are learning:

1. What book language sounds like.

Remember that written language is a different dialect from that spoken by your students. More formal, usually written in the standard English dialect, book language is what they will gradually learn to write. It is not the familiar language that they speak with their family and friends. Before they can be expected to produce this written dialect, they need to hear it, to begin acquiring that dialect of English in much the same manner that they earlier acquired the ability to speak English.

2. Forms that writing can take.

As students listen to language or read it, they also gain knowledge of the forms (schemata) through which they can express their ideas. Through listening to novels or short stories, for example, students are developing a "sense of story." They are learning how an author engages characters in dialogue and how character traits are revealed through behavior. They are introduced to such concepts as theme, setting, and plot development. Sharing other forms—haiku, song lyrics, an editorial, a letter of complaint—helps students learn how to write those forms.

3. Grammatical structures.

As students listen to good writing, they hear a variety of sentence structures. They hear sentences composed of varied combinations of clauses, phrases, and strings of words. They are adding to and reinforcing their knowledge of English grammar as they listen to the opening sentences that William Saroyan wrote for *The Human Comedy*, speaking in the third person of the omniscient author:

> The little boy named Ulysses Macauley one day stood over the new gopher hole in the backyard of his house on Santa Clara Avenue in Ithaca, California. The gopher of this hole pushed up fresh moist dirt and peeked out at the boy, who was certainly a stranger but perhaps not an enemy. Before this miracle had been fully enjoyed by the boy, one of the birds of Ithaca flew into the old walnut tree in the backyard and after settling itself on a branch broke into rapture, moving the boy's fascination from the earth to the tree.

4. Feelings, ideas, content.

A good book presents interesting content, vicarious experiences, and ideas that students can talk and write about. The characters share emotions with which they can identify. Students gain insight into the lives of others and begin to understand the concepts of diversity and universality applied to the people with whom they inhabit the earth.

5. The sound of fluent reading—intonation.

As you read, students hear what fluent reading sounds like. They hear the accents and pauses, the intonation that a good reader uses automatically. They can talk about the meaning that intonation adds to language. They are learning to enjoy reading and talking about good books together.

6. The joy of reading; what books have to offer.

Less able readers may be hearing a book that they could not read independently whereas able readers are often motivated to read a book that you have shared. All enjoy the experience of sharing an engaging story, laughing together, or even sharing the vicarious experience of death. The students are developing positive attitudes toward reading through your enthusiastic sharing.

Every piece of literature—every example of writing—that we share through reading aloud teaches students more about language and literature. Your reading aloud, however, offers additional assets as a teaching strategy of which you should be aware. One important advantage is that reading an article, a short story, or the chapter of a book means that *the whole class has a body of shared content that all can respond to immediately*. Your teaching is not hampered by students who have not read the assignment or completed their homework. Nor do you have to locate a class set of books. Reading aloud is *efficient and economical*.

Furthermore, reading aloud is *very enjoyable*. A sense of *camaraderie* develops through this shared experience—a *rapport* between you and your students that benefits the total learning program you present.

As you select literature to share with students, keep these tips in mind:

- Choose books or other forms of literature that interest you. You cannot project enthusiasm unless you truly feel it.

- A humorous selection is usually a sure winner and a good choice for beginning a Read-Aloud Program.

- Include multicultural literature that increases students' empathy and knowledge of other ethnic groups.

- Present some of our classic literature that is part of our shared heritage. Reading aloud often serves to make some of these books more palatable and comprehensible to contemporary students.

- Choose different forms of literature so that students become aware of the characteristics of varied genres of writing.

- Include writing from different fields, for example, science or history, so that students recognize that literature and writing are in all fields of study.

Here are a few selected titles that you might choose to begin reading to your students:

Grades K–2:

Where the Wild Things Are by Maurice Sendak

The Snowy Day by Ezra Jack Keats

Madeline by Ludwig Bemelmans

Blueberries for Sal by Robert McCloskey

The Biggest Bear by Lynn Ward

Sam, Bangs, and Moonshine by Evaline Ness

The Happy Owls by Celestino Piatti

Crow Boy by Taro Yashima

A Bear Called Paddington by Michael Bond

Mother Goose by Tomie dePaola (poetry)

The Dead Tree by Alvin Tresselt (science)

Grades 3–7:

The Borrowers by Mary Norton

The Twenty-One Balloons by William Pene duBois

The Cricket in Times Square by George Selden

The High King by Lloyd Alexander

The Light Princess by George MacDonald

The Wind in the Willows by Kenneth Grahame

The Genie of Sutton Place by George Selden

Mrs. Frisby and the Rats of NIMH by Robert C. O'Brien

Homer Price by Robert McCloskey (short stories)

The Phantom Tollbooth by Norton Juster

Where the Sidewalk Ends by Shel Silverstein (poetry)

Dragonwings by Laurence Yep (historical novel)

Grades 7–9:

The House of Wings by Betsy Byars

The Return of the Twelves by Pauline Clarke

The Hobbit by C. S. Lewis

A Wrinkle in Time by Madeleine L'Engle

Watership Down by Richard Adams

Ishi by Theodora Kroeber

The Perilous Gard by Elizabeth Pope

Where the Lilies Bloom by Vera and Bill Cleaver

A Gift of Watermelon Pickle edited by Stephen Dunning and Ed Lueders (poetry)

Black Boy by Richard Wright (history, autobiographical)

Grades 9–12:

The Pigman by Paul Zindel

I Know Why the Caged Bird Sings by Maya Angelou

The Doll's House by Henrik Ibsen

Spoon River Anthology by Edgar Lee Masters

Lord of the Flies by William Golding

Go Tell It on the Mountain by James Baldwin (history)

Bless Me Última by Rudolfo Anaya

Gift from the Sea by Anne Morrow Lindbergh

Celebrations: A New Anthology of Black American Poetry edited by Arnold Adoff

The Medusa and the Cell by Lewis Thomas (scientist; essays)

SMALL-GROUP TALKING ABOUT IDEAS

A natural way to begin small-group discussions is to begin with the literature you have just shared. Students do need direction, however, in order to work successfully in small groups.

For example, after reading the first chapter of *Dragonwings* by Laurence Yep, an excellent novel about the Chinese men who came to California in the early twentieth century, aloud to a group of fifth-grade students, you might direct them to work in groups of four to compose a list of questions about what they have just heard. Questions might include a wide range of difficulty levels, such as:

1. What is the Golden Mountain?

2. How will Moon Shadow feel about meeting his father?

After the groups have composed their lists of questions, have them take turns asking a question to the class. After answering a number of questions, discuss why some questions were easy to answer and others were more difficult. Point out the levels of thinking required to answer specific questions. In this way, you are helping your students become aware of the thinking processes they are using (metacognition), which is an important aspect of learning.

Then write two of the more interesting questions on the board. Direct the students to copy one question to write an answer to as homework to share the next day. Tell the students that this sharing will be done in small groups. Not only do students enjoy this interaction but it also exerts social pressure for each student to come prepared. Each group can select one answer to share with the whole class. They can then identify the qualities that made these answers better than others, thus rediscovering together how to answer questions more effectively the next time.

Notice that all students can participate in this activity at their individual levels of ability. This activity integrates thinking with listening and speaking. It also supports the reading program and prepares students to express their thinking about literature through writing, which is an effective prewriting activity. Furthermore, this group activity can be used following any presentation of literature, for it is a learning experience that bears repeating.

Talking in small groups prepares students for evaluating and editing writing in small groups. Students do need to learn how to work effectively as members of a group, so a discussion will be helpful. Have students generate rules that will help them work in groups more productively, and present the rules on a chart, as shown.

Working in Groups

1. One person should not talk all the time.
2. Everybody's ideas should be accepted. We shouldn't laugh at what anybody suggests.
3. We should stick to the topic and not begin talking about personal things.
4. Having a group leader might help us remember the rules or we could all remind each other.

Cooperative learning groups may be formed for varied purposes focusing on varied tasks or topics, for example:

Problem solving

Story telling

Planning a presentation

Brainstorming ideas

Collaborative learning

Teaching by an "expert"

Clustering group knowledge

Conversations

As students work in groups, they are learning language by using it for specific purposes. These aural-oral activities engage students in thinking as they learn to participate in group efforts. Such involvement moves naturally into the writing of language as students record ideas, assign tasks, or write a report of their group planning to share with other students in the class.

IDENTIFYING WHAT STUDENTS KNOW ABOUT LANGUAGE

As you begin working with a new class, you may wish to talk with them about your intent to focus on language and literacy, discussing the skills and content covered by both terms. Think of your time with this class as a research study with your hypothesis being, perhaps: "I can increase each student's ability to think and to write." Your job, then, is to design intervention strategies that will achieve your objective, that is, to make this hypothesis a fact.

A positive first small-group activity focuses on the students' discovery of how much they already know about language. This preassessment also provides a group benchmark for your research, even if no one else ever sees the results. This collaborative effort draws from the collective knowledge of the group. After that base is established, students reach out to discover more, and they will continue this study through the year.

SAMPLE LESSON

TITLE: Exploring Language as a Way of Communicating

LEVEL: Grades 4–12

TIME REQUIRED: 2–4 weeks

OBJECTIVES:

Students will:

1. Become aware of the language they speak

2. Engage in a search for information

3. Work in cooperative learning groups

4. Compile a report of information

PROCEDURES:

Stimulus

Address a question to one of your students, for example, "How are things going with you today, Josie?" When the student replies in English, ask, "What language are you speaking, Josie?" Repeat with several similar questions to other students.

Then make the comment, "In this class we speak English. Some of you know other languages, but the language we are using to communicate is called English. What do you know about language? Why do we need language?" Elicit ideas from the class. (They probably won't have too much to say.)

Next say, "It sounds to me as if we need to find out more about language since we use it every day."

Divide the class into groups of four or five students. Direct the groups to begin brainstorming for ten minutes as they take turns listing ideas about language. Ideas will vary widely, for example:

We speak English.

Language is the way humans communicate.

People in different countries speak different languages.

We use words when we talk.

Animals have languages, too.

Language can be oral or it can be written.

Somebody is teaching a chimpanzee to talk.

Birds can talk, too.

Language can be funny.

Writing language is hard.

Don't try to predict what students will generate at this stage, but do know that they will become involved in this process because our language is something everybody is interested in. After ten minutes, ask the groups to share their ideas. Taking one from each group in turn, have several recorders write the ideas on the chalkboard. After all are recorded, have students examine the ideas to see which ones are related.

Ask each group to select one of the categories of ideas about language to investigate further. For instance, groups might focus on:

Animal Languages

The Different Languages in the World

Why English Is Our National Language

How Humans Communicate

Humor in Our Language

Why Writing Is Hard

Talk about the different ways of discovering information about the selected topics. Of course, we want students to go to the library, but guide them to create a list that includes other methods of investigating a topic, for example:

Library

Books about language
Articles in magazines, *Readers' Guide*

Interviews

> Parents, family, friends
> Librarians
> Local experts
> Each other

Letters

> Authors of books
> Publishers

Telephone calls

> Libraries
> Publishers
> Experts

The groups can begin their more focused work by brainstorming again, expanding their list of ideas. They can also list ways of beginning their research.

Brainstorming and planning will require one full period. You may wish to plan lessons on such techniques as conducting and writing interviews or writing letters, each of which will require one full period. You may plan a period for guided research in the library. Student groups will need to do some work outside of class. (Refer to the list of materials related to this topic in the Appendix.)

Writing Activity

Have students collect the results of this collaborative research and present it in a formal report that includes the four major parts of a research study:

1. Statement of the Problem Studied

2. Outline of Procedures—Chronology

3. Summary of Findings

4. What We Have Learned through This Research

Students can share their reports in any manner they choose: drama, a radio report, a videotaped presentation, and so on.

Postwriting

These reports can form the nucleus of a class book entitled "What We Know about Language." As students extend their work on language, help them continue to clarify what they are learning about language. Have them make additions to this class resource book which will grow with them. At the end of the semester, you might have students write individual papers on what they have learned about language.

SUMMARY

In order to function adequately as writers, students need to dev lop facility with spoken language. They need to sort out their ideas a d discover that they have something to say. They also need to feel t ease in constructing varied sentences to communicate meaning orally before we can expect them to generate successful sentences in writing. Thus, listening and speaking will continue to be very much a part of the writing process as students exercise their brains and begin formulating their ideas. By engaging with oral language, students are developing an "ear for language"—the knowledge of English grammar and idiom—that will enable them to generate and evaluate written language successfully.

Introducing Evaluation and Editing Concepts

Our first emphasis in writing is always on having students record their ideas, developing fluency (ease) with writing. We don't want students to be hampered by that Eagle-Eyed Editor looking over their shoulders as they write. Students who are overly concerned about "correctness" are literally afraid to write because they might make a mistake. Therefore, we encourage beginning writers to write by using invented spelling, pictures, or any way of conveying meaning in writing.

Once they begin writing, of course, the students will want to make their writing public. Displayed on the bulletin board, published in a class anthology, sent to parents as a gift, their writing should be dressed appropriately for the occasion. We can guide students to polish their writing before they send it out in the world alone.

Remembering that editing is a broad term that includes all aspects of improving one's writing, we can show students how to apply specific editing techniques.

BASIC EDITING STRATEGIES

Gradually introduce students to editing skills that are used by all writers. These same strategies are used whether we write in pencil, with a pen, or at the computer with a word processing program. Notice that these strategies are closely connected to evaluation.

Students should begin editing as an ongoing, formative part of the writing process—something they do for themselves as they write. Later, some of the same techniques will be employed as they edit each others' writing.

Suggest three basic components of editing that will be repeated, as needed, throughout the writing process. Students should check all three before asking someone else to respond to their work.

Editing Check 1:   Read your work aloud to check grammaticality.

If a sentence follows English grammar rules, it will flow smoothly. "Does it sound right?" is a valid question for English-speaking students to ask as they read their writing. Reading their work aloud helps students check their sentences against that "ear for language" we have been talking about. Listening to their sentences helps students develop their writing ability by:

1. Becoming aware of awkward idioms (expression).

Is that really what we say?

2. Noticing the lack of transition (choppiness).
   Identify words that aid the flow of ideas.

3. Discovering unfinished sentences or ideas (clarity).
   Consider the audience.

Guide students to recognize that as they critique their writing, as described, they are evaluating it at that stage. Evaluation should be seen as an ongoing process, not just a grade placed on a completed product.

Editing Check 2:   Read critically for clarity.

The purpose of writing is to communicate to a reader. Therefore, clarity is an important objective that students should constantly test. Is what I have said clear? Am I saying what I mean to say? Students might record their writing at a Listening Center in order to enable them to listen to it more critically, distancing themselves from the writing they have been so personally engaged in.

Encourage students to think particularly about the audience for whom they are writing. When writing a story, they should work to describe the setting in sufficient detail so the reader can really picture that place. In an essay, they should take a strong position and substantiate their arguments, trying to persuade a reader to agree with their viewpoint. In explaining a process, they want to be sure they did not leave out an essential step in the procedure so the reader can follow the process exactly. This sense of audience is essential to effective writing.

Working on clarity will be helped greatly by peer response, as we will discuss in the next section.

Editing Check 3:   Scan for surface errors.

Students need to develop the skill of scanning the surface of the paper to see that sentence markers are in place and that paragraphs are indented. Student-created checklists described in the next chapter will be helpful for this purpose.

Point out that skillful proofreaders do not read the content. If they become involved with the content or ideas, they miss punctuation and capitalization errors.

Notice, too, that proofreading is the least important of these editing processes. Anyone can correct such surface features as spelling and form. The good writer gets paid for the ideas in a poem, a well-structured plot in a short story, or a clear explanation of a process in an article. On the other hand, we writers who do not have secretaries or copy editors to check our work must do this job for ourselves because sloppy surface features turn off readers who then may never read our work. Mechanical errors can also cause confusion about the meaning we want to convey.

PEER EDITING PROCESSES

Reading each other's writing proves beneficial to both reader and writer. Students learn more about writing as they see the kinds of ideas other students have and how they develop them. Student writers benefit from the questions and suggestions of their fellow students—real readers who appreciate their efforts but who may also have trouble understanding an idea they are presenting. We try to establish a sense of responsibility for each other in the workshop so that students learn to assume the roles of learner and teacher, in turn, as they work together.

Step I: Begin with Pairs

The easiest way to move into group work is to have students form partner teams. You may choose to assign partners in order to pair stronger with weaker students or, at other times, pairs of like abilities. In general, you will want to change partners frequently so that students have experience working with different people in the class.

As with any group work, students need a clear sense of purpose and expectations. Explain that your purpose in having them work in pairs is to help each other work on specific writing tasks (perhaps using the analogy that two heads are better than one).

Before moving into editing tasks, you might have students work in pairs for other activities, for example:

1. Conversations in Writing: Students converse about topics that interest them. With no talking permitted, they must take turns writing and reading the response.

2. Collaborating on a Tall Tale: The pair of students answer the questions: Who? When? Where? What? and Why? After identifying the characters, setting, and some rudiments of a plot, they begin writing a tall tale.

3. Active Listening: Have students talk in pairs. Each takes a turn telling a memory story from childhood while the other listens. After each minute or so, the teller stops talking. The listener then restates what the partner said. The story teller corrects inaccuracies. After about ten minutes, the roles are reversed.

These kinds of cooperative learning activities demonstrate how collaboration works. Students can learn to listen to each other, to ask questions, and to consider the partner's feelings in developing a product together.

Working on editing tasks, then, is a natural progression. After any writing activity, students can work together using the same techniques that they have already used on their own work, for instance:

- Reading each other's work aloud to check for grammaticality, flow, and transition.

- Reading the work carefully to see if it is clear, if they understand what the writer is saying.

- Scanning the work for surface errors—form, spelling, mechanics.

To encourage students to put efforts into the editing task, we often have student editors sign their name at the end of the paper, noting that the work has been edited. Then, if gross errors are discovered later, the editor is equally responsible.

In editing, too, we talk with students about using all of the resources available, listing suggestions collectively on a chart to remind students of ways they can obtain information.

Ways of Finding Out

1. Look in the dictionary for spellings and meanings.
2. Ask another student. (Limit 3 during a period.)
3. Use other reference books in the classroom, for example, the English textbooks.
4. Find out at home or from a neighbor.
5. Go to the library.
6. Ask the teacher. (Limit 1 per day.)

Working in pairs will continue to be helpful even after students have begun working in small groups. Discuss ways that students can help each other during the writing process, encouraging them to ask for help when needed and to provide supportive assistance for others. For example, a writer may need to read a piece of writing to an audience to check on clarity even though pairs have not been formally established for that purpose.

Step II: Response Groups

A response group consists of four or five students who usually work together for several weeks. Discourage students from asking to change groups until everyone regroups; students need to learn to get along with varied people to perform a given task. Sometimes these groups are designated as *families* to emphasize the supportive interaction expected of members of the group.

Beginning activities for groups must be nonthreatening so that all students can participate readily. Lead up to editing activities gradually, thus:

1. Working in pairs will facilitate moving smoothly into response groups, as described in the preceding section. Many students find the one-to-one interaction easier to handle at first.

2. For the first response group activity, have students number off by five to form a random selection of students. Initiate the first meeting of these groups after students have written any short piece that they can share, for example, a personal

narrative or a familiar story told from a different point of view. Have students move into groups and sit quietly to hear the directions. They are to take turns reading their stories. Then each group is to select one story to share with the large group. By repeating this activity several times with other writings, students will soon discover that writing for each other is enjoyable and that their fellow students like to hear what they have written. Help them become aware of what they are learning about writing by hearing how others handled a specific activity.

3. The next time students write, move closer to the editing process by directing each student in the group to point out one especially good feature in each person's writing after it is read. It is important at this stage that responses remain positive.

4. The next step is to have each member of the audience point out one good feature and then suggest one idea for improving the writing. By now, students should feel fairly positive and secure about having their friends respond to their writing even by offering helpful suggestions.

The main thing to remember in introducing group editing techniques is to progress in small increments so the tasks are manageable. Instruction, of course, will support the growth of student knowledge about aspects of writing which will then be emphasized in student editing.

SUMMARY

At all levels of instruction students can begin to value the strengths of their writing while at the same time learning specific ways to improve their writing abilities. The skillful writing teacher will engage students in such simple editing strategies as reading their sentences aloud to check the grammaticality. Students will learn that proofreading for surface errors is only important after the ideas are expressed clearly enough to communicate meaning to the reader. Editing and evaluation will be used frequently as part of the formative growth of the novice writer. Students will work individually, in pairs, and in collaborative small groups as they help each other learn to write for varied purposes.

Instruction to Support Editing

Young writers need to keep learning more about the process and the craft of writing. Instruction naturally supports students' gradually developing editing skills. Teaching might be planned to help students in the following manner:

1. Students who are having consistent problems with clarity may need to reinforce their ability to explore ideas more fully before writing, for example, employing the clustering technique.

2. Discussing the qualities of good writing will help students develop a checklist that will remind them of specific ways of improving their own writing. This list also suggests comments they can make to help other students.

3. Demonstrating the revision process with the whole class working on one paper displayed on an overhead projector will help students see just how editing takes place and what they can look for in their own writing and that of other students.

CLUSTERING TO CLARIFY THINKING

Clustering is an effective device for organizing information about a topic. We begin with one word or topic in the center of our paper. We then add associated ideas around it as they come to mind. As we brainstorm ideas, they tend to cluster in categories, as shown in Figure 3–1. The ideas, of course, come from the individual writer's brain. One diagram may produce the content for a paragraph or a poem.

Figure 3–1. Example of Clustering

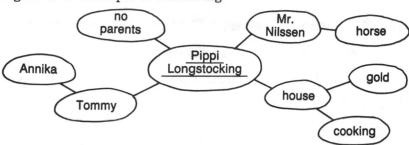

Clustering shows us what we know about a topic as well as what we don't know. It can be used for both pre- and postassessment. For example, after students have read a book, clustering will help them outline an oral or written review of the book. The main character may be the focus, as in Figure 3–1 based on *Pippi Longstocking* by Astrid Lindgren (Viking).

Having students begin research with the development of one or more clustering exercises will help them assess their own interest in the subject(s) they first thought of studying. Clustering also points up what they already know and what they need to find out. Beginning, thus, with subjects that interest them, students should investigate sources beyond the encyclopedia. As they gain additional information, they can fill in the initial outline suggested by their original clustering.

Supervising this process for weaker writers will assist them in clarifying their own thinking before they begin to write.

IDENTIFYING THE QUALITIES OF GOOD WRITING

What is good writing? What does a writer do that makes his or her writing worth reading? Even young students have definite answers to these questions.

As a way of helping students discover the characteristics of good writing, have the class as a whole generate a list of what they think good writers do. A group of third-graders might suggest ideas like these:

Good writers:

1. Use interesting words

2. Begin sentences with capital letters

3. Write about exciting adventures

4. Spell words right

5. Write long sentences

A high school group will probably include some of the same ideas, but they may phrase them differently:

Good writers:

1. Use colorful adjectives to describe a setting so the reader can picture it clearly

2. Vary the way sentences begin

3. Grab the reader's attention right away

4. Know how to punctuate sentences, particularly dialogue

5. Find out how to spell words they want to use

Because these lists reflect your students' knowledge at a particular time, they provide a benchmark for the class—a place to begin. The list should grow, changing as the students learn more about writing through reading and their own experience. The class that produced the first list will, no doubt, learn that good writers often use very short sentences to contrast with those long ones, so they will need to amend that quality of good writing.

The list provides criteria against which students can always assess their own writing before exposing it to someone else's view. These ideas also suggest specific aspects of writing that student editors can refer to as they respond to the writing of other students.

Instruction should be directed toward clarifying students' recognition of aspects of writing that concern expert writers—stylistic devices, imagery, word choices, humor, and so on. As you read writing aloud, you will guide students to observe examples of especially effective writing. Periodically, ask the class if they need to change or add any items on their checklist based on this new information. Thus, the list grows, reflecting student knowledge.

It is important to observe one important detail about this teaching strategy. *The process of discovering ideas and generating the checklist must be done anew with each group.* One group of students generates the ideas listed as they are discovered; they own that list and therefore try to implement it. We cannot impose the list generated by one class on another and expect the procedure to work equally well. Nor can we impose a list published by Professor Noah Word, no matter how knowledgeable he is about the technicalities of fine writing. As students engage in writing activities, they are thinking, discovering insights, and internalizing what they have learned: That is the learning process that we want to nurture.

REVISING A PAPER COLLECTIVELY

Reproduce two or three student papers on overhead transparencies to use as demonstrations of the revision process. Choose papers that display aspects of writing that you may want to feature, for example, paragraph development, parallelism, or the interview as a writing form. For anonymity, remove the name of the student author or use papers from different classes. After a workshop atmosphere has been established, students will usually not mind having the class work on their papers.

Occasionally, you may need to create a paper that shows what you want students to focus on. At other times, you may reproduce examples of excellent writing, perhaps featuring the use of metaphor. This way of working together can also be used to present or to review ideas that the whole class seems to be unsure of, for example, the use of clustering or the Venn diagram, even developing a paragraph or an essay collectively to show students just how the process works.

Reflection

The ability to revise and edit writing depends on the writers' knowledge of the English language—idioms, grammatical structures, vocabulary, and the like. Therefore, a good writing program continuously supports students' English language acquisition by including oral activities that engage students in thinking, listening, and speaking before, during, and after writing. We teach students how to evaluate and edit their own writing and that of other students as a way of learning to write. Rethinking the teacher's role in teaching writing removes the responsibility for copyediting student work, which is a heavy paperload that defeats the need for frequent student writing. Instead, we develop a collaborative workshop approach to teaching writing that is enjoyable and effective. We build on what students already know and guide them to discover and experiment with emulating the good writing styles they observe in literature.

Challenge

Begin preparing to use the ideas presented in this chapter.

1. Select several books that you think students in your class might enjoy. As you read each book, keep an *Assessment Journal* in which you note the progress of the plot, ideas for teaching, and activities that come to mind. Mark the pages of your notebook in columns, thus:

   Title of Book: _____

Page	Plot Events	Ideas	Learning Activity

Under *Ideas*, note interesting quotes, imagery, outstanding sentences, provocative content, or any other teachable feature.

2. Cluster around a topic that you might develop into a unit of study in your classroom, for example: Problems Our Country Faces, Hispanic Culture in Our Community, or Getting Along in Today's World. Jot down ideas about how the unit would work with students, what your objectives will be, and what activities you might plan. Find out what resources are available to support this study.

3. Think about your own ability and knowledge about writing. Visit a university library or purchase a book or two to learn more about writing so that you can better facilitate student writing. The list at the end of the chapter suggests appropriate titles.

4. Form a writing group with several of your colleagues. Arrange to meet once or twice a month to share writing and to talk about the qualities of good writing as you help each other learn. No one has to be an expert!

Exploring Further

Kroll, Barry M., and Vann, Roberta J. *Exploring Speaking-Writing Relationships: Connections and Contrasts*. National Council of Teachers of English, 1981.

Petersen, Bruce T., ed., *Convergences: Transactions in Reading and Writing*. National Council of Teachers of English, 1986.

Rico, Gabriele L. *Writing the Natural Way*. Tarcher, 1983.

Smith, Frank. *Writing and the Writer*. Holt, 1982.

Strunk, William, and White, E. B. *The Elements of Style*, 3rd ed. Macmillan, 1979.

Sudol, Ronald A., ed. *Revising: New Essays for Teachers of Writing*. National Council of Teachers of English, 1982.

Tiedt, Iris M. et al. *Teaching Writing in K–8 Classrooms: The Time Has Come*. Prentice-Hall, 1983.

Willis, Meredith Sue. *Personal Fiction Writing: A Guide to Writing from Real Life for Teachers, Students, & Writers*. Teachers and Writers Collaborative, 1984.

4

Integrating Evaluating and Editing Activities into Language Arts Instruction

Books aren't written, they're rewritten. Including your own. It is one of the hardest things to accept, especially after the seventh rewrite hasn't quite made it.

Michael Crichton

As students progress in their ability to read and write, they should become more and more aware of *the writing they read*. We can plan integrated lessons that take full advantage of student interest in an intriguing short story by Roald Dahl or in a provocative essay from *Time*, guiding students to identify the features of effective writing modeled in literature. We can also lead students to observe student-written literature in the same way, identifying stylistic devices they appreciate or writing that flows smoothly with an obvious effort to include transitional elements that carry the reader along. Thus, both reading and writing abilities develop with a clear sense of connection between the process of producing writing and the reading of someone else's writing. Through reading, students are preparing to edit and evaluate writing that they and their peers produce.

In this chapter we will focus on planning evaluation and editing of writing as an integral part of a rich language arts context. These integrative activities engage students in listening to and reading varied types of literature. They also stimulate thinking, talking, and writing in response to literature. Through such learning experiences students become excited about learning, and they do learn! We will note, too, that these activities are essential for students who are less able readers and writers, perhaps students "at risk," as well as the students who perform well above grade level.

After completing this chapter, you should be able to:

1. Plan activities that engage students in observing the skillful use of language in literature they read

2. Guide students to identify the characteristics of specific types of writing

3. Guide students to write various types of writing

4. Plan revising activities for students

5. Help students prepare their writing for publication

6. Introduce students to varied ways of presenting their writing in book form

Reading Literature to Learn to Write

Obviously, students learn to write by writing, but they also learn to write by reading. Usually, students who are good readers almost automatically become good writers. They have rich vocabularies and sufficient knowledge from which to draw, and they have absorbed a sense of story that enables them to write a narrative with relative ease. They have some experience with expository forms and are able to present an argument with reasonable support. These students are ready to move toward perfecting their writing, exploring varied purposes for writing, and appreciating the writing of others.

Students who are less able readers need to read more frequently and increase their fluency with reading, gradually becoming self-motivated to read with enjoyment. Yet, these students can also begin to observe literature as a way of learning to write. They need the same rich experiences with literature that we provide for more able learners. And they need the same stimulus to express their thinking in writing.

In the preceding chapter we emphasized reading aloud to all students as an effective way of seeing that everyone has the opportunity to know good literature. We will continue to present literature orally to the whole group during prewriting activities as well as encourage their independent reading at whatever level they can manage. Good books are available for all levels of an individualized reading program. Students are learning to read and to write as they share the writing of these experienced authors.

As we read together, we will guide students to respond to the literature they read, entering into a transaction with this author-person who is sharing ideas. Our objectives at this stage of working with student writers include:

- Making students aware of the author as a person who has ideas to share

- Inviting students to enter into a transaction with each author they encounter

- Exposing students to varied forms of writing and helping them to identify the features characteristic of distinct forms of discourse

- Teaching students about specific stylistic devices and other aspects of writing that they observe in literature models

- Planning lessons that engage students in learning more about the craft of writing

Selecting Different Forms of Discourse

We can deliberately introduce varied forms of discourse in our literature reading and writing program to ensure that students have some familiarity with a range of types of writing. We might well begin with the varied types of writing identified by Moffett.[1]

**Thinking Up
(Imagination)**

   Fiction
   Plays
   Poetry

**Looking Back
(Recollection)**

   Autobiography
   Memoir

**Noting Down
(Notation)**

   Journal
   Diary

**Thinking Over/
Thinking Through
(Cogitation)**

   Column
   Editorial
   Review
   Personal Essay
   Thesis Essay

**Looking Into
(Investigation)**

   Biography
   Chronicle
   Case
   Profile
   Factual Article
   Reportage and Research

It is interesting to note that the types of discourse listed here do not include some of the forms we may be accustomed to teaching, for example, the paragraph or the five-paragraph essay. Emphasis in Moffett's types appears to be on the ideas expressed rather than the form of presentation.

In 1986, the Educational Testing Service worked with teachers and researchers to select from Moffett's modes of discourse the following eight types of writing to emphasize in a first statewide assessment of writing abilities of eighth graders in California in the spring of 1987.[2]

1. Report of Information
   The writer collects data from observation and research and chooses material that best presents a phenomenon or concept.

2. Eye Witness Memoir
   The writer tells about a person, group, or event that was objectively observed from the outside.

3. Autobiographical Incident
   Narration of a specific event in writer's life and stating or implying the significance of the event.

4. Firsthand Biography Sketch
   Through incident and description the writer character-
   izes a person he/she knows well.

5. Story
   The writer shows conflict between characters or between
   a character and the environment including dialogue and
   description.

6. Analysis—Speculation About Effects
   The writer conjectures about what may result from a specific event, cause and effect.

7. Problem Solution
   The writer describes and analyzes a specific problem and
   then proposes and argues for a solution.

8. Evaluation
   The writer presents a judgment on the worth of an item—
   book, movie, artwork, consumer product—supported with
   reasons and evidence.

The types of writing specified reflect the intent of the author
and ways of thinking rather than prescribed poetry or prose forms.
For example, a report of information could be a resume or a book
review. A story might take the form of a fable or an extended dialogue. Thus the emphasis is not so much on producing a specific
form as it is on the expression of students' ideas for a specific purpose.

PLANNING INSTRUCTION TO INTRODUCE VARIED
TYPES OF WRITING

How can we introduce such varied kinds of writing to students who
may not be familiar with these types? Of particular interest in the
statewide assessment mentioned in the preceding section are the
strategies recommended for teachers to use in preparing students
to perform well. Discovery methods invite students to examine student-written or literature models of each type of writing in order to
identify features of the type of writing to be produced, as described
in the following lesson plan.[3]

LESSON PLAN

TITLE: Introducing Students to the Book Review

TYPE OF WRITING: Report of Information

LEVEL: Grades 3–12 (Adjust material and expectations.)

OBJECTIVES:

Students will:

1. Read a book review

2. Identify characteristic features of this form

3. Write a book review that includes these features

PROCEDURES:

Locate the review of a book that you would like students to know or perhaps an author you would like to introduce. Duplicate a class set of copies of the review. Included at the end of this lesson plan is an example of a book review you could use for the elementary grades and the high school.

Stimulus (Prewriting)

Give students copies of the book review you have selected. Read the book review aloud slowly as students read their copies. (This is especially helpful for students who are less able readers and ESL students, and it helps keep the class together for purposes of the lesson.)

Then have students return to the beginning of the review and direct them to identify the kinds of information the author included in the review. Begin a chart, Features of a Book Review, as students list such characteristics as the following:

Features of a Book Review

1. Includes quotations from the book

2. Comments about the content presented by the author

3. Tells something about the author, biography

4. Expresses personal reaction to the book

5. Includes the title, author, publisher, and year

Direct the students to bring a book that they have already read to class the next day.

Activity (Writing)

See that each student has a book to review. Display the Features of a Book Review list that the class compiled. Go through the lfeatures one by one with the class as students take notes based on the books they are reviewing.

Tell students to complete the first draft of the book review they have begun as homework.

Follow-Up (Postwriting)

On the next day students should have the first drafts of their book reviews and copies of the book to be reviewed. Have students work in groups of three to five students. Each student is to read his or her book review aloud as the others listen to see if all features on the list have been included. After listening to a review, each member of the group should answer the following two questions for that writer:

1. What one aspect of this review was especially well written?

2. What one recommendation would help improve the writing?

Each student should mark the writing that was commended with a big star. The writer should also take notes on the suggestions for improvement to aid revision.

Students should complete a revision of this first draft as homework that night. They should bring both the first draft and the revision to class.

The next day revised versions of the book reviews can again be shared in the same editing groups. Each writer should point out exactly what changes were made from the first draft. Any further changes should be made, as needed.

Evaluation

Before completing the final draft of the book reviews, students should work as a class to determine just how these reviews will be evaluated. They might consider these types of evaluation:

- Pass or Fail (based on what is being taught)

    10 points   The completed book review contains all of the features listed.

    0 points   The completed book review does not contain all of the features listed.

- A Simple Rubric or Standard (some recognition for excellence)

    10   Uses excellent detailed description
         Shows clear personal involvement
         Includes important biographical information
         Speaks clearly to the audience
         Includes all features listed, very well-presented
    5   Presents all features adequately
         Needs further revision
    2   Presents most features, very weak writing
         Needs extensive revision

Students who are involved in determining evaluation measures for their own work are assuming responsibility for their work. They also have clear ideas of what they need to do to get the top score, and they can help each other so that potentially everyone in each group can get the top score. Thus the teacher moves out of the authoritarian role of Grade Giver.

Students can also implement the scoring, reading each paper to see which score it deserves. Students learn much about writing by reading each other's work. They are also engaged in thinking as they evaluate each other's writing.

When book reviews are fully revised, they can be published instantly in a three-ringed notebook that bears the title: Books We Recommend. Have someone decorate the cover. This collection, containing something by everyone in the class, should be available in the classroom for reading. Later, it can be shared with others by placing the collection in the library.

Following are student examples of weak and excellent writing that received the scores of 10 and 2 in the lesson described. The excellent review could be used as the stimulus for initiating the lesson as students identify the features of a good book review.

Weak Book Review: Jacob Have I Loved

I read *Jacob Have I Loved* by Katherine Paterson. It was a good book from start to finish. The story is told by Sara Louise. She grows up on an island where most people fish. She becomes a nurse and gets married to a man who has three children. I think anyone would enjoy reading this book.

Well-Written Book Review: Where the Red Fern Grows

Wilson Rawls was a country boy from the Ozarks. He spent much of his time roaming the hills with a blue tick hound, hunting and fishing, enjoying the out of doors.

It was natural, then, for him to write a book about a boy who wanted hunting hounds, a boy who also roamed the hills and river bottoms of the Cherokee country so familiar to Rawls. He describes the setting, thus:

> Our home was in a beautiful valley far back in the rugged Ozarks. The country was new and sparsely settled. The land we lived on was Cherokee land, allotted to my mother because of the Cherokee blood that flowed in her veins. It lay in a strip

from the foothills of the mountains to the banks of the Illinois River in northwestern Oklahoma.

Where the Red Fern Grows is a story of love for family, for animals, and for this country. It is also a story of adventure as Billy achieves his greatest dreams.

Ten-year-old Billy wanted a pair of coon dogs, but hounds cost more money than the family could possibly afford. Determined, Billy began saving his money, storing it in an old K. C. Baking Powder can. After almost two years, he had fifty dollars, enough to buy the two redbone coon hound pups that would change his entire existence.

Billy, Dan, and Little Ann spent their lives together from the time he brought them home. As he said:

> It was wonderful indeed how I could have heart-to-heart talks with my dogs and they always seemed to understand. Each question I asked was answered in their own doggish way.
>
> Although they couldn't talk in my terms, they had a language of their own that was easy to understand. Sometimes I would see the answer in their eyes, and again it would be in the friendly wagging of their tails. Other times I could hear the answer in a low whine or feel it in the soft caress of a warm flicking tongue. In some way, they would always answer. (page 68)

The high point of the book is Billy's winning the gold championship cup in the annual coon-hunting contest. With the cup came a large cash prize that answered his mother's prayers for a new house.

Billy continued to hunt with his dogs until one night they met the "devil cat of the Ozarks, the mountain lion." His brave little dogs tried to save Billy from the lion whose "yellow slitted eyes burned with hate." Although Billy finally killed the huge animal with an ax, the dogs were badly wounded. Old Dan died from his injuries, and Little Ann soon died, too, of heartbreak at losing her hunting companion. Billy sadly buried the two dogs in a beautiful spot on the hillside.

As the family was leaving the Ozarks the following spring, Billy ran to this grave for one last farewell. It was then that he saw the beautiful red fern that had sprung up above the graves of the little dogs. He remembered the old Indian legend that said "only an angel could plant the seeds of a red fern, and that they never died; where one grew, that spot was sacred." As they drove away, the family could see the red fern "in all its wild beauty, a waving red banner in a carpet of green."

Fast action, human interests, and believable characters make this a book for readers of all ages. A master storyteller, Wilson Rawls has shared a piece of himself.

SUMMARY

One way that students learn to write is by reading the writing of others. We can guide them to read varied types of writing and to identify the main features of a specific type of writing. After discovering the features, students can use the features list to guide their attempts to write that type of writing.

We use strategies that involve students actively in observing writing that someone else has done as a way of learning how to write more proficiently. Thus, students are engaged in discovering aspects of writing they can understand and can try themselves. Because they understand the features of the writing they are composing, they can also determine appropriate ways of evaluating the success of their attempts at writing a specific type of writing. Thus, students are thinking about writing, reading, analyzing, and evaluating writing, and then applying the information gained as they write themselves.

Revision, Rethinking, and Rewriting

In our writing workshop we will continue to talk with students about the writing process and questions that arise as they are writing. We will encourage students to become aware, too, of their own thinking (metacognition)—new experiences, problem solving, insights—that may occur as they write. Knowing how few students observe adults writing anything longer than a grocery list, we will also model the writing process ourselves and share the problems that we too have with writing.

LOOKING ANEW AT THE WRITING PROCESS

Students are writing daily in some form or other. They write many short in-class pieces that are shared in small groups, and occasionally they write longer pieces that are partially completed as homework. It is time to give serious attention to revision and what it means.

Talk with students about how we go about developing a first draft into a polished paper that warrants publication. Review the steps presented in Chapter 1:

Step 1:   Reading and Rereading (orally and silently)

Step 2:   Revision: Rethinking, Reshaping, Rewriting

Step 3:   Preparing the Final Copy (written carefully in ink, set in type, or printed with the computer)

Step 4:   Proofreading (to catch the surface errors)

Step 5:   Publication

Talk about each of these steps in detail, allowing students to ask questions and to discuss each step in turn. Note, too, that each of these steps can be done alone, in pairs, or in larger editing groups.

Step 1: Reading and Rereading

Have students talk about the reasons for reading their writing aloud. What are they checking for? Compile a class list of specific things to check during this first step in the revision process, thus:

- Grammaticality: Does each sentence sound "right"?

- Flow: Do sentences flow smoothly along? Does each idea flow naturally into the next?

- Sentence Variety: Are sentences of different lengths? Do they begin in different ways?

- Repetition: Is the same word used too often?

- Vivid language: Can an interesting word replace a dull one?

- Clarity: Is each sentence clearly stated? Is each part of a process or argument described clearly?

- Usage: Are words used precisely?

- Audience: Does the writing speak directly to a specific audience?

Step 2: Revision: Rethinking, Reshaping, Rewriting

Discuss the activities appropriate to this stage. Help students recognize that substantive changes must be made during revision; make it clear that proofreading is not their concern during this stage. Students can add suggestions to their revision guide, for example:

- Organization: Will a reader immediately see the order and be able to follow it easily? Does the organization fit the topic presented? Do sentences and paragraphs follow an appropriate sequence?

- New Ideas: Has something important been omitted? Could another fresh idea be added? Will readers find the writing interesting?

- Sentence Combining: Can two or more short, choppy sentences be combined into a more mature, better-written sentence?

- Style: Are the sentences written with a touch of style, wit, and imagery? A certain freshness of expression?

Encourage students to "cut and paste" or to edit freely with a word processing program and the computer. Always have them save their first drafts to compare as they progress toward the final copy.

Step 3: Preparing the Final Copy

After revision has been completed, students will prepare the final copy of the manuscript. At this stage, their manuscript is ready to be made public in some way. Discuss the reasons for taking the trouble to polish writing carefully before sending it out into the world alone.

The final copy may be neatly written with a pencil (for the younger writers) but older students will probably use a pen. Students can also use a typewriter. In the next section on publication we will also discuss artful ways of enhancing writing by incorporating calligraphy and illustration with the text.

As often as possible, students should use the word processor to prepare a really professional looking printed copy of their revised writing. Using the computer is not only motivating, but it also enables students to edit easily. Students are more likely to revise at greater depth with the computer because making major changes is relatively easy compared to erasing or rewriting pages of material. There is no inherent value in struggling with handwriting if a computer is available.

Step 4: Proofreading

The word *proofreading* has often been used as a synonym for editing. Proofreading, however, means exactly what this compound word denotes: *reading proof.* The proof is a printed copy of the writing as it has been set in type or print. An editor reads the proof to catch surface errors—omitted words, spelling errors, transposed letters, and other typos. Today, of course, we can proofread our manuscript on the computer before we actually print hard copy.

The proofreading stage is the last chance to catch errors before going to press. Students can help each other proofread in order to catch mistakes that might detract from the effectiveness of their writing when it is published.

Step 5: Publication

Publication contains the word *public,* so publication means making writing public. Ways of making writing public include simple methods of displaying the writing on the bulletin board, informal classroom collections of writing, and more formally bound journals or anthologies of student writing. In the last section of this chapter we will explore varied publication methods. Publication does provide an incentive for working through the revision steps we have just described.

STRATEGIES FOR ENCOURAGING REVISION

Revision is an ongoing process that happens as an integral part of writing. Thus, revision should not be seen as a linear activity that we deal with only when we have finished a piece of writing. Make it plain that writers often stop to read and to think about what they have written, and that they make changes as they go.

Talk with students about how you write as you work on an article during the writing workshop periods. Be sure that the students see you scratching out lines or even whole paragraphs and making arrows to remind you to move a sentence into a paragraph below. Make it clear to students that a neat first draft doesn't show evidence of much thinking. Praise students who really rework their writing visibly. You may even plan an ostentatious crumpling of paper as you groan and throw away a page of writing that just didn't work.

A TOUCH OF HUMOR

Older students may appreciate reading the following humorous sentences created to make a point about grammar or usage. Students may need to talk about some of the examples in order to understand the point being made.

Never split infinitives, but to occasionally split one is possible.

I will avoid ending sentences with a preposition unless it is already written down.

Always and assiduously avoid alliterations.

Avoid using mixed metaphors like a plague of locusts.

Students may write other rules like these to share. To write them, of course, they must understand the aspect of language on which they are basing their humor.

EXPANDING SENTENCES

A mark of immaturity in writing is repeated use of short simple sentences. As students gain fluency with spoken language and have greater exposure to literature, they usually begin writing sentences of varied length. You may wish to provide exercises designed to encourage them to include more detail in their sentences. Ask students to write five two-word sentences that contain only a noun and a verb, such as:

> Cats purr.
>
> Dogs bark.
>
> Cars honk.
>
> Flowers bloom.
>
> Stairs creak.

Then ask the students to share their sentences. Choose one sentence to expand. Demonstrate on the board with the students' help. Underline the two-word sentence, as shown:

> In June I love to visit my grandmother, who lives in Santa Cruz, to see how luxuriantly the *flowers bloom* in her garden, roses near the house because they smell so wonderful, tall hollyhocks along the fence, and marigolds that reflect the sun.

Have students count the number of words in the expanded sentence. (43) Comment on the detail that is now included which helps you really visualize the garden. Note the kinds of information that have been added—time of year, where the grandmother lives, kinds of flowers, and a brief description of each flower.

Challenge students to see who can write the longest expanded sentence. (This is a great homework assignment!) Have students make a list of the information that was added, for example:

Time of day

Place

Month, year

People, size, shape, identity

How something is done (adverbs)

Color

Smells

Tastes

Textures, feel

Sounds

Feelings, emotions

After students share their long sentences, display one written by each student on a bulletin board where others can read them. Repeat this motivating activity several times.

SENTENCE PATTERNS

Help students become aware of the varied patterns of English sentences. You might choose to focus on simple sentences in which the predicate is expanded, thus:

Pattern I: N V (Subject/Predicate) Horses eat.

Pattern II: N V N (Subject/Verb/Object) Horses eat hay.

Pattern III: N LV Adj (Subject/Linking Verb/Complement) Horses are hungry.

Pattern IV: N LV N (Subject/Linking Verb/Complement)
Horses are workers.

Pattern V: N V N N (Subject/Verb, Direct Object/Indirect
Object) Horses give us rides.

Have students write their own examples for these five patterns.
This is a good way to introduce some of the grammatical labels: noun,
verb, linking verb, adjective, subject, predicate, object, complement,
direct object, and indirect object. Once the terms are introduced in
context, you can reinforce students' knowledge of the terms by using
the words as you talk about sentences they are writing.

You may also have students search literature for examples of
each of the identified patterns. Display the examples on a bulletin
board with a column for each pattern. Again, students will be interested in reading the examples found, noting the books in which
they appeared.

COMBINING SENTENCES

Sentence-combining activities can be fun as students try to discover
ways of putting sentences together in more inventive ways. To introduce the technique, write two simple sentences on the board, such
as:

Bill bought a bicycle.

The bicycle was red.

Challenge the students to put all of these ideas into one sentence.
You might want to underline the ideas that are important in each
sentence, for example:

Bill—the owner of the bike

bought—what he did

bicycle—what he bought

red—description of bike

If we can write a sentence that contains all of these ideas, we have combined two simple sentences into one more effective sentence, thus:

Bill bought a red bicycle.

Most students will have little difficulty with this exercise, so you can move on to combining simple sentences:

Mary likes to swim.

Jane likes to swim.

When students combine these sentences to form a compound subject, they will have to change the verb form, thus:

Mary and Jane like to swim.

Here is an opportunity to point out the difference in the singular and plural verb forms in the third person in English grammar. Ask students: "How did you know that these verb forms are different?" (This is only one of the many examples of the internalized knowledge of English grammar that native English speakers share.)

Continue combining sentences in this manner. Invite students to write two or three simple sentences and to challenge a neighbor to combine them. In this way they are thinking and writing as they engage in providing their own examples once they see how combining works.

Provide students with a longer piece of writing on which they can work to combine sentences. Everyone has the same story, but the results will be different. You might challenge students to see how tightly they can combine the sentences so that they have as few sentences as possible. Here is one story you might use with your students:

Molly Whuppie

Once upon a time there was a man and a wife. They had too many children. They could not get meat for them. They took the three youngest. They left them in the wood.

The children travelled and travelled. They could see never a house. It began to get dark. They were hungry. At last they saw a light. They made for it. It turned out to be a house. They knocked at the door.

A woman came to it. She said: "What do you want?"

They said: "Please let us in. Give us something to eat."

The woman replied: "I can't do that. My man is a giant. He would kill you."

They begged hard. "Let us stop for a little while. We will go away before he comes."

She took them in. She set them down before the fire. She gave them milk and bread. They began to eat.

A great knock came at the door. A voice said:

> "Fee, fie, fo, fum,
> I smell the blood of some earthly one.
> Who have you there, wife?"

"Eh," said the wife, "It's three poor lassies. They are cold and hungry. They will go away soon. Don't touch them, man."

He said nothing. He ate a big supper. He ordered them to stay all night.

Now he had three lassies of his own. They were to sleep in the same bed with the three strangers.

The youngest of the three strange lassies was called Molly Whuppie. She was very clever. She noticed that before they went to bed the giant put straw ropes round her neck and her sisters'. Around his own lassies' necks, he put gold chains. Molly took care. She did not fall asleep. She waited. She was sure everyone had fallen sound asleep. She slipped out of the bed. She took the straw ropes off her own and her sisters' necks. She took the gold chains off the giant's lassies. She put the straw ropes on the giant's lassies. She put the gold chains on herself and her sisters. She lay down again.

It was the middle of the night. Up rose the giant. He was armed with a great club. He felt for the necks with the straw. It was dark. He took his own lassies out of bed. He battered them. They were dead. He lay down again. He thought he had managed well. Molly thought. It was time she and her sisters were off and away. She wakened them. She told them to be quiet. They slipped out of the house. They all got out safe. They ran and ran. They never stopped until morning.

They saw a grand house before them. It turned out to be a king's house. Molly went in. She told her story to the king.

He said: "Well, Molly, you are a clever girl. You have managed well. You could manage better. Go back. Steal the giant's sword that hangs on the back of his bed. I will give your eldest sister my eldest son to marry."

Molly said she would try. She went back. She managed to slip into the giant's house. She crept in below the bed. The giant came home. He ate a great supper. He went to bed.

Molly waited. He was snoring. She crept out. She reached over the giant. She got down the sword. It was over the bed. It gave a rattle. Up jumped the giant. Molly ran out the door. She had the sword with her. She ran. He ran. They came to the Bridge of One Hair. She got over. He couldn't.

He said: "Woe worth ye, Molly Whuppie! Never come here again."

She said: "Twice yet I'll come to Spain."

Molly took the sword. She gave it to the king. Her sister was married to his son.

Well, the king he said: "Ye've managed well, Molly. You could manage better. Steal the purse. It lies below the giant's pillow. I will marry your second sister to my second son."

Molly said she would try. She set out for the giant's house. She slipped in. She hid again below the bed. She waited. The giant had eaten his supper. He was snoring sound asleep. She slipped from under the bed. She slipped her hand below the pillow. She got out the purse. She was going out. The giant wakened. He ran after her. She ran. He ran. They came to the Bridge of One Hair. She got over. He couldn't.

He said: "Woe worth ye, Molly Whuppie! Never come here again."

"Once more yet," quoth she. "I'll come to Spain." So Molly took the purse. She gave it to the king. Her second sister was married to the king's second son.

After that the king said to Molly: "Molly, you are a clever girl. You could do better yet. Steal the giant's ring. He wears it on his finger. I will give you my youngest son for yourself."

Molly said she would try. Back she went to the giant's house. She hid herself beneath the bed. The giant came home. He ate a great big supper. He went to his bed. He was snoring loud. Molly crept out. She reached over the bed. She got hold of the giant's hand. She pulled. She pulled. She got off the ring.

The giant got up. He gripped her by the hand. He said: "Now I have caught you, Molly Whuppie. If I had done as much ill to you as ye have done to me, what would ye do to me?"

Molly said: "I would put you into a sack. I'd put the cat inside with you. I'd put the dog with you. I'd put a needle and thread and a shears in. I'd hang you up upon the wall. I'd go to the wood. I'd choose the thickest stick I could get. I would come home. I'd take you down. I'd hang you till you were dead."

"Well, Molly," said the giant. "I'll do just that to you." He got a sack. He put Molly into it. He put the cat beside her. He put the dog beside her. He put in a needle. He put in thread. He put in shears. He hung her up upon the wall. He went to the wood to choose a stick.

Molly sang out, "Oh, if ye saw what I see."

"Oh," said the giant's wife. "What do ye see, Molly?"

But Molly said never a word but "Oh, if ye saw what I see!"

The giant's wife begged. She wanted Molly to take her up into the sack. She wanted to see what Molly saw. Molly took the shears. She cut a hole in the sack. She took out the needle and thread with her. She jumped down. She helped the giant's wife into the sack. She sewed up the hole.

The giant's wife saw nothing. She asked to get down again. Molly never minded. She hid herself at the back of the door.

Home came the giant. He had a great big tree in his hand. He took down the sack. He began to batter it.

His wife cried. "It's me, man." The dog barked. The cat mewed. He did not know his wife's voice.

Molly came out from the back of the door. The giant saw her. He ran after her. He ran. She ran. They came to the Bridge of One Hair. She got over. He couldn't.

He said, "Woe worth ye, Molly Whuppie! Never come here again."

"Never more," quoth she, "will I come again to Spain."

Molly took the ring to the king. She was married to his youngest son. She never saw the giant again.

SENTENCE VARIETY

Have students turn to a book they are reading to observe the writing of that particular author. Ask students first to count the number of words in all of the sentences on the first two or three pages of the book. Lead students to generalize that good writers use sentences of varied length.

Someone may observe that an author used a two-word sentence. Help students recognize reasons for occasional use of a very short sentence in their writing. The short sentence provides a pleasant contrast. A short sentence may also be used to achieve a specific effect, for example, surprise or definite conclusiveness.

Have students examine a selection of their own writing and count the number of words in each sentence. Then have them revise that selection using sentence combining and expansion techniques to create sentences of varied length. Immediately, their writing should become more interesting to read.

For a second lesson on sentence variety ask students to examine a piece of literature to see how many different ways the author began a sentence. Have the class compile a list, such as:

How Sentences Begin

I went home after school.

In the morning we went fishing.

Leaping into the water, John rescued the child.

When I told him my story, he shook his head in disbelief.

If students suggest sentences that follow the same structure as another on the list, write that one below the other so students can begin to recognize the grammatical constructions. You may wish to identify each construction, for example, pronoun or prepositional phrase, but don't overemphasize learning these labels. However, do encourage students to incorporate these varied constructions in their writing following the examples on the chart displayed on the wall. Gradually, they will learn the grammatical terms as they use them to discuss their writing.

Display a sample of writing in which every sentence begins in the same way, thus:

I was only five when we left Ohio. I liked living there. I liked going fishing with my dad. I have many friends in Ohio. I have aunts and uncles there, too. I would like to go to Ohio again to visit.

Note that this writing sounds monotonous. Point out that this writing is typical of younger writers. Suggest ways to add sentence variety.

Have students examine a selection of their own writing to see how many different ways they have begun sentences. Ask them to revise the writing following the examples listed on the chart. You might challenge students to write a story in which every sentence begins with a different construction.

Keep adding examples to the list of sentence beginnings as students discover others. This is a marvelous way to discover many aspects of English grammar which is largely in the syntax of sentences.

REVISING COLLABORATIVELY

Use the overhead projector to focus on sentences from the students' own writing. Select sentences that could be expanded or combined to support instruction that has preceded, for example:

John went to the store.

He bought a loaf of bread.

Students can suggest ways of combining these simple sentences, for instance:

John went to the store to buy a loaf of bread.

Notice that there is no single right answer. Encourage students to consider various ways of working with the sentences you present to make them more interesting and effective.

You may present a paragraph or a longer work on which the class can work together as they consider larger ways of revising writing. For example, invite students to revise this piece of anonymous student writing:

An Anxious Moment

All morning I sat waiting for the mailman to come. Why doesn't he come, I thought.

Everyone else had received their invitation yesterday. I felt terrible. What if the mailman came and there wasn't an invitation?

Mother, seeing my anxiety, suggested that I clean up my room while I was waiting. That way the time would pass faster.

At last the mailman arrived. I ran to the door and grabbed the mail before he dropped it in the box. Quickly, I sorted through bills and ads. It had to be there, that long blue envelope. It had to be! It was.

Insert the changes suggested by students—adjectives, adverbial phrases, whole sentences—work on it collaboratively. Write the improved version on another transparency and remove the editing marks from the original transparency. Then compare the two versions to see the results of editing.

SUMMARY

Introduce students to revision gradually. Learning such skills as sentence combining is more effective when it grows directly out of a student-identified need. Collaborative learning activities can focus on sentences and paragraphs taken from student writing. Drill-type exercises should certainly be minimized. Having students examine literature as an example of writing will lead them to recognize the many connections between reading and writing, between composing and comprehending, and to view themselves as real writers.

The most effective way of teaching various aspects of good writing is through discovery methods that invite students to observe and identify features of a type of writing and to select aspects of writing that they recognize as more interesting. Through discovery they assume responsibilty for their own learning and for applying what they have discovered. Students enjoy revising writing for which they see a purpose—writing that will be published.

Publishing Student Writing

Writing is hard work. But seeing your name in print somehow makes up for all the effort put forth.

We need to guide students to write for real purposes. They can write learning logs, letters of inquiry, narratives based on family history, and reports of information they have discovered. Writing for real purposes lends an incentive for revising their work, for polishing it well before it is made public. Students need to see writing as a powerful way of communicating with other people in the world.

We can also reinforce the value of student writing by offering opportunities to publish their writing. Even simple publication methods enhance students' writing and provide incentives for polishing their work. Every student will benefit from having his or her best writing published.

In this section we will first enumerate types of writing that engage students in writing for a public. We will also describe various ways of helping students publish their writing.

WRITING TO COMMUNICATE

Writing serves a real function in the world. Invite students to write as a way of participating in local, state, and world events. You might begin by making a list of the kinds of writing that people do in the real world, such as the following example.

People write:

Grocery lists

Letters to the editor

Thank you notes

Diaries

Addresses, telephone numbers

Directions

Orders from a catalog

Requests for information

Reports for a committee

Birthday greetings

Applications for a job

Have students examine a real form of writing, for example, letters to the editor. As outlined in the sample lesson presented on page 102, have students identify the features of a good letter to the editor based on their observations. Then ask them to write a letter to the editor (or to the principal or the cook) about a real issue that concerns them. They should then mail these letters and expect to get a response. Keep adding to this list of writing that people really do as students discover different kinds of writing.

WRITING BOOKS TO SHARE

Helping students publish their writing in book form adds stimulus to writing. Every student can become a published author. Student-published books are wonderful products to share with parents at an Open House or to place in the school library where other students can admire the work of each author. Following are a variety of ways to publish in book form, from the very simplest to the more complex.

Instant Publication in Class

Any time students write something together, you can guide them to revise their first drafts and to place their revised work in a collection of class writing. Described here are several ways of publishing student writing instantly and painlessly.

- *I Remember Stories* is the title printed on the front of a three-ringed notebook. Students place their revised personal narratives in this notebook as soon as they are completed. Every student has a story included. One student may write a Table of Contents while another decorates the cover of the book. The book is placed on a reading table where class members may read the stories. Later, the book is donated to the school library where other students may enjoy it, too.

- Students are writing haiku as part of a unit on Japan. Each child selects one poem to publish in a volume, writing directly on a ditto master.

Each student receives one copy of the booklet to present to his or her parents as a holiday gift. The cover is decorated with a Japanese-style blown-ink design of cherry blossoms on a dark branch.

- Students who are reading *Wind in the Willows* can write character descriptions and draw pictures of the characters and their home for a class collection: *Who's Who Along the River*. Two students could work on a fold-out map of the river country locating each character's home.

Any collection of student writing can be instantly bound by adding two sheets of colored construction paper as covers for the book and stapling the volume together. Students can write their short selections on ditto masters if you want to provide a class set of the books to share with others in the school and community. Run the stories back-to-back to save paper.

Accordion Books

Simple binding ideas permit students to present their writing in a decorative manner. The accordion book can include as many pages as you wish. Decide on the size of the pages of the book, and then make a long strip of paper which can be folded accordion-fashion to produce the page size desired, thus:

Accordion books work well for a simple continuous child's story or a series of poems written by a student poet. Students may also use this format for a collection of favorite quotations or proverbs from different countries.

Binding Books

A fascinating writing project is the creation of children's books. Written by the students, the books are published in hardbound form—the next thing to a commercial publication.

The stories may be retellings of old fairy tales, original fables, or modern myths; they may be realistic stories about characters with problems or humorous tales of the misdoings of a contemporary trickster. The source of story material is endless.

As students prepare to write children's books, they should examine some of the marvelous books that have been published during the past years. (Examining these books is a good way to induce older students to read the children's literature they may have missed.) Go to your local library to locate some of the following titles to share with students:

Joseph's Yard by Charles Keeping (Oxford)

In a Spring Garden edited by Richard Lewis and illustrated by Ezra Jack Keats (Dial)

Puzzles by Brian Wildsmith (Watts)

Grabianski's Wild Animals by Janusz Grabianski (Watts)

Thumbelina by Adrienne Adams (Scribner)

One Fine Day by Nonny Hogrogian (Macmillan)

The Soldier and the Tzar in the Forest trans. by Richard Lourie and illustrated by Uri Shulevitz (Farrar)

The Nightingale by H. C. Andersen, trans. by Eva LeGallienne and illustrated by Nancy E. Burkert

The Gondolier of Venice by Robert Kraus and illustrated by Robert Byrd (Windmill)

Theodore and the Talking Mushroom by Leo Lionni (Pantheon)

Everyone Knows What a Dragon Looks Like by Mercer Mayer (Four Winds)

Demeter and Persephone by Barbara Cooney Porter (Doubleday)

The Angry Moon by William Sleator and illustrated by Blair Lent (Little)

These are just a few of the wonderfully illustrated books for children. You might arrange a field trip to the library to browse through the picture book section of the public library. If you take your class there, do explain the project your class is undertaking and invite the children's librarian to select a number of outstanding books to share with your students.

Have students identify the features of an excellent book for young people. They can list such features as:

Effective content in children's books should:

> interest young children
> present original ideas
> depict characters realistically and honestly
> include appropriate emotions, not sentimentality
> be comprehensible to young children
> incorporate a distinctive style of language

Effective illustrations in a book for children should:

> suit the content of the book
> be understood by children
> support or extend the story content
> represent excellent art in varied media
> avoid stereotyped art and ideas[4]

After exploring children's books, students can brainstorm ideas for books they can write. They will need to spend time writing and revising their stories. They should also decide how the print will be placed on the page and how many pages they will require. Illustrations of some kind should be part of the publication.

Students of all ages enjoy binding books with semi-hardbound covers. The materials you need for this project are:

Cloth or paper for covers of book

Tablet backs for covers

Plain or figured wrapping paper for inside covers

White typing paper for pages

Long stapler or darning needles and heavy thread

Drymount paper or paste

Scissors

Several electric irons

Colored pens and other art materials for illustrations

Older students can follow these directions and complete their books with a minimum of supervision. Younger students will need assistance.

1. Run two long pieces of masking tape vertically between the two pieces of cardboard on the front and back.

2. Cut the cover material (wallpaper, cloth, contact paper, wrapping paper, or other suitable material) to cover the entire cover, with an extra inch all around.

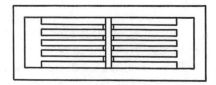

3. Fold the material down and paste it on all sides.

4. To put the leaves into the book, staple the pages. Cut two strips of paper the length of the book and four inches wide and fold them in half. Paste one-half of the folded strip on the front cover and the other half on the stapled pages. Do the same thing with the back of the book.

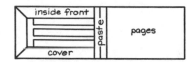

5. To give the inside a neat, finished look, cut two pieces of paper for the front and back inside covers about one-fourth inch smaller than the cover and paste them in place.[5]

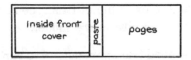

Students should also include the following in their books:

Copyright information

Title page

Table of contents (if appropriate)

Dedication (if desired)

Information about the author

Index (if appropriate)

The important thing about writing a children's book is sharing it with an audience. Arrange to have your class read their books to a group of younger students. The books could be displayed for a PTA meeting or in a local library. Students may want to donate their books to a library where they can be read by others.

SUMMARY

Publication lends stimulus to the writing process. Students of all ages enjoy seeing their signed work in print. Parents also appreciate seeing their child's writing enhanced with art. Through publishing activities, from the simple to the more complex, we demonstrate value for student writing and help students explore their creativity in varied media.

Challenge

Prepare for classroom activities by following these directions.

1. Follow the lesson plan modeled in the first part of the chapter. Select one specific type of writing to introduce to students. Locate an example of this type of writing. Plan your lesson around this literature model.

2. Prepare overhead transparencies you can use in introducing the different ways of varying sentences described. Plan lessons using these transparencies. Be sure to include student discoveries of writing in the literature they are reading in your plans.

3. Follow the directions for publishing student writing. Make a sample of each of the types of publications described. These samples will be useful in directing a publication project in your classroom.

Endnotes

1. James Moffett. "Kinds of Writing." Workshop at San Jose State University, June 30, 1986.

2. California State Department of Education. *Writing Assessment Handbook, Grade 8,* 1986.

3. Iris M. Tiedt. *Lessons from a Writing Project.* David Lake, 1987. The SAFE Model for planning lessons.

4. Iris M. Tiedt. *Exploring Books with Children.* Boston: Houghton Mifflin, 1979, p. 34.

5. From Tiedt / Bruemmer / Lane / Stelwagon / Watanabe / Williams, *Teaching Writing in K-8 Classrooms: The Time Has Come,* © 1983 Prentice Hall, p. 199. Reprinted by permission of Prentice Hall, Inc. Englewood Cliffs, New Jersey.

Exploring Further

Clapp, Ouida. *On Righting Writing: Classroom Practices in Teaching English.* National Council of Teachers of English, 1975.
De Beaugrande, Robert. *Writing Step by Step.* Harcourt, 1985.
Graves, Donald. *Teachers and Children at Work.* Heineman, 1983.
Harris, Muriel. *Practice for a Purpose.* Houghton Mifflin, 1984.
Kirby, Dan, and Liner, Tom. *Inside Out: Developmental Strategies for Teaching Writing.* Boynton/Cook, 1981.
Tiedt, Iris M. *The Language Arts Handbook.* Prentice-Hall, 1983.

5

Teaching the Conventions of Writing

Writing is hard work. It's hard work for the first-grader and for John Steinbeck and for all of us in between.

John Sweet

The conventions of writing cover a wide variety of matters on which there is general agreement or consensus. At the same time, since conventions may also be somewhat arbitrary, there is considerable disagreement or confusion about certain practices. The important ideas to remember are:

1. Conventions are general agreements about how writing should be presented. These agreements are opinions that range over a period of time. As such, these opinions are subject to change.

2. Conventions of writing are surface features that include varied groups of information, for example:

   Punctuation
   Capitalization
   Spelling
   Usage
   Form

3. Conventions are less important than the ideas a writer expresses, so we encourage young writers to put their thoughts

on paper before worrying about surface features. Lack of attention to the conventions can, however, affect communication and may also prejudice the reader against the writer.

We need to discuss the conventions of writing with students. In general, we agree that worrying about making errors in punctuation or spelling should not be allowed to interfere with the creative process. Therefore, we will not stress "error avoidance." On the other hand, we must make students aware of the high value many members of our society place on spelling and using words "correctly."

In this chapter we will examine the mechanics (punctuation and capitalization), spelling, usage, and form as well as methods of proofreading for surface errors. In each section of the chapter we will outline concepts students should learn, and we will talk about instructional strategies for the classroom.

After reading this chapter, you should be able to:

1. Discuss ways of helping students discover punctuation and capitalization practices used in writing English

2. Plan lessons that engage students in learning more about the conventions of writing

3. Help students overcome difficulties with spelling

4. Guide students to handle matters of form in writing

5. Teach students how to proofread for surface errors

6. Discuss conventions of contemporary usage

Teaching the Mechanics

The mechanics of writing focus on the details or routine procedures. When teachers refer to the mechanics, they usually mean punctuation and capitalization. Defined thus, the mechanics are rightfully deemphasized during the first draft stages when student writers are trying to clarify their thinking and to express their ideas in writing.

The mechanics, then, can be seen as the surface features to be checked during the final drafting of a paper and during the proof-reading stage of the writing process.

First of all, you might ask students to consider why we mark our sentences following conventional practices of punctuation and capitalization, and even why we divide concepts into words. Have students try to read this writing that contains no markings to help the reader:

> ifidontuseanypunctuationandcapitalizationatallyoutheread
> erwillhaveaterribletimeunderstandingjustwhatiwanttoco
> mmunicateyouprobablywillgiveupandreadsomethingthatispro
> perlyspacedwithcommasandcapitalsintheirplacestohelpyouf
> indyourwayaroundthesentencesevenmycomputerisconfusedab
> outwhentoendawordsoitjustkeepsgoinglettingwordssplitwh
> eretheywill

Writing with no concern for the reader's task certainly slows down the reading process, making it as difficult as possible! Therefore, it is easy to lead students to generalize reasons for following conventional practices of separating words, punctuating sentences, capitalizing some words, and even spelling words according to accepted conventions. We are trying to communicate clearly to our readers, and we want to remove any obstacles that get in the way of communicating our meaning.

PUNCTUATION

Students may be interested in investigating the evolution of current practices of punctuation. As with spelling, in earlier years punctuation practices were determined by the writer or printer, so that we can find interesting ways of punctuating.

The early Greeks used a semi-colon where we now use a question mark:

Where are you going;

An early printer, William Caxton, used slashes to separate sentences and periods to mark the end of paragraphs, thus:

we will come to the school on saturday to clean up the school yard/if everyone helps it wont take long/we will all benefit from having an attractive campus. on the following saturday we will work on marking the playground for games we all like to play/ the home and school club is furnishing the paint and other supplies.

As printing developed and more and more books were being printed, conventions of punctuating written language became more regular. Aldus Manutius, a book maker referred to as the father of modern punctuation, is credited with formalizing practices of punctuating sentences.[1]

Punctuation practices are still evolving, however. Writers in the seventeenth and eighteenth centuries used punctuation marks much more frequently than we do today. We tend to simplify punctuation, omitting marks unless they are really needed. For example, contemporary practice omits the following marks that you may have been taught to use:

1. A comma before the *and* in a series.

   Pablo purchased ground beef, cheddar cheese, lettuce and tortillas to make tacos.

2. A comma before the zip code in an address.

   Sarah lives at 147 Via Rosalinda, San Jose, California 95128.

3. A comma separating the city from the two-letter postal abbreviation for a state.

   Jeffrey Watson
   1289 South Martin Drive
   Champaign IL 61820

It is interesting to note that many people resist such changes and may even state that such practices are wrong. Our conventions sometimes become so strongly internalized that we find it difficult to change what is familiar. Language changes often remain in flux for years before finally gaining wide acceptance.

Changes in handling punctuation happen gradually, of course, and are few in number. The number of symbols we use in punctuation has also been relatively stable through the years. Although not widely used, the first innovation in punctuation since the seventeenth century is the *interabang*, a cross between the question mark and the exclamation mark, invented for use with questions that really aren't questions, thus:

"What do you make of that ?"

"Now, how do you like that ?"

Obviously the study of punctuation has a place in any writing program, and this study can be both functional and interesting. We recommend the following attitudes and practices in working with punctuation conventions:

1. *Never use* workbook pages or duplicated sheets of isolated punctuation exercises. Such drill teaches students nothing except that English is a dull, boring subject.

2. *Do use* discovery methods that engage students in finding out how real writers use punctuation marks in the literature they read. (We know that publishers' editors deserve some of this credit, but for our purposes we'll give it to the authors.)

3. *Avoid* being overly "uptight" about any conventions of writing. You can almost always find examples of writers who do not follow the rules you may have learned. For example, many writing handbooks state adamantly that contractions should not be used in formal writing. You don't have to look very far in respected periodicals and texts, however, to find examples like the one in the sentence you are reading and those that follow:[2]

We don't know who the speakers are . . . and we can't ask them for clarification.

Geoffrey Nunberg, *Atlantic*

. . .others aren't, and that's that.

Linda Flower
Problem-Solving Strategies for Writing

4. *Do* include a little humor in the study of mechanics. For instance, note how the meaning changes with the punctuation:[3]

Don't! Stop!
Don't stop!

Seventy-nine and thirty are the winning numbers.
Seventy, nine and thirty are the winning numbers.

5. Have students observe the connection between punctuation and intonation (pauses, rising and falling pitch) as we speak. For example, ask students to suggest possible punctuation for the following:

why are you giving him that candy
mrs harley bought a car coat and velvet pants
mary ann judith marie and kathy joe are friends

6. Stress functional punctuation used in the context of student writing. Help students discover skills they need.

The lesson presented here involves students in searching for varied uses of common punctuation marks. The objective is to prepare a Class Writer's Handbook that will become part of each student's writing notebook.

A SAMPLE LESSON

TITLE: Discovering Punctuation

LEVEL: Grades 2–12 (Adapt difficulty of literature selections to student abilities.)

OBJECTIVES:

Students will:

1. Perceive literature as writing

2. Observe punctuation used in a literature selection

3. Express rules for using common punctuation marks

4. Compile a set of punctuation rules they can follow

PROCEDURES:

Direct students to bring a book they are reading to class. A class set of the same book or a set of basal readers could be used. Prepare a transparency or duplicated copies of a short narrative to be used for demonstration. You might use the following fable by Aesop (you may rewrite to simplify the punctuation for younger writers).

The Hare and the Tortoise

Hare insulted Tortoise on account of his slowness and vainly boasted of her own great speed in running.

"Let us have a race," replied Tortoise. "I will run with you five miles for five pounds, and Fox there shall be the umpire of the race."

Hare agreed, and away they both started together. But Hare, an arrogant braggart, outran Tortoise to such a degree that she made a jest of the matter. "Ho, ho," she shouted, "that tortoise will never make it this far!"

Deciding to rest awhile in the sun, she squatted in a tuft of fern that grew by the road, closed her eyes, and took a nap, thinking that, if Tortoise went by, she could at any time catch up with ease.

In the meantime Tortoise came plodding along with slow but continued motion. Hare, who felt overly secure and confident of victory, overslept. So, the tortoise crossed the finish line first, thereby winning the five pounds!

Moral of the Story: The race does not always go to the swiftest.

Stimulus

Tell students you are going to read a piece of writing to them. Display a short narrative on an overhead transparency and read it to the class.

Tell the students you want them to observe how this writer punctuated the sentences in the narrative. Have students read the sentences aloud one-by-one as you discuss the punctuation used and the reason for using that marking.

Begin a chart on a big sheet of mural paper, on which to record class findings, thus:

Using Punctuation Marks

Periods	*Commas*	*(Add other columns needed)*
At end of sentence		

Add different uses of each mark as they are observed. After completing the collaborative observation, ask students which uses of punctuation were most common. They may observe that the comma is used more frequently than other marks—even more often than the period.

You can use whatever words students use to describe reasons for using specific punctuation or you may wish to supply technical terms, for example, clause, series, or appositive, without particular discussion. The example will identify the feature for students.

Activity

Have students work in groups of three to five members as they search the writing they have before them to discover different uses of punctuation, especially uses other than those already listed. Each group should have one person serve as the recorder to note the mark, the sentence in which it appears, and the reason for using the punctuation.

After approximately fifteen minutes, have each group report one finding to the class. Have a student from each group enter that finding in the appropriate column on the chart.

Follow-Up

Leave this chart on the board for the next week. Talk to the class about continuing the search individually as they read independently. Invite them to share each morning as you add information to the chart.

Then plan the making of a Class Punctuation Handbook. Each student can prepare an assigned page, thus:

Comma

Use Number 2:

Rule: Use a comma to separate words in a series.

Examples:

There was a knife for sharpening the pencils, and india-rubber for rubbing out anything which you had spelt wrong, and a ruler for ruling lines for words to walk on, and inches marked on the ruler in case you wanted to know how many inches anything was, and Blue Pencils and Red Pencils and Green Pencils for saying special things in blue and red and green.
Winnie-the-Pooh, page 159

We slept in the same room, ate at the same table, sat for nine months out of each year in the same classroom, but none of these had made us close.
Jacob Have I Loved, page 58

Prepared by:
_____

Each student can be the expert on the rule for which he or she prepared the handbook page. A student who needs information about punctuating a series can go to the person whose name appears at the bottom of that page.

One or two students can prepare a Table of Contents for the book. Another can decorate a cover. Students should duplicate the pages, collate them into books, and staple the books together. Each student will then have a class-made reference book to place in his or her writing notebook. Copies of this book could be sold or given to other students or parents who would like individual copies.

Evaluation

Students should evaluate the project by summarizing what they learned by completing this activity. Encourage them to consider the full process rather than just enumerating specific punctuation rules. Guide them to recognize the thinking that went into the project, the exposure to literature, and the writing of different authors.

Your monitoring of this project at all stages of development shows you the level of involvement for each individual student. Note that the value of this activity is as much in the process as it is in the final product.

Discovery methods pay off far better in terms of student learning than the read-and-test methods that we often use. Students who have discovered themselves how punctuation marks are used internalize many understandings as they search for examples. Because they produced the pages for the book, they are likely to apply the information the class collected, and they will enjoy referring to the handbook to remind themselves of applications they may forget.

CAPITALIZATION

Punctuation serves a real function for the reader, but it is more difficult to establish a rationale for capitalization. Capitalizing the first word in a sentence certainly serves as a sentence marker that assists the reader, and perhaps we could safely say that capitalizing proper nouns helps connote their importance. Most of the rules for capitalizing, however, are somewhat tricky and must be memorized through use and discussion.

Use the same discovery methods recommended and described for punctuation. Begin with what students already know and what they can discover through observation. Have them categorize the information, thus:

First words

> Sentences
> Titles (plus other important words and the last one)
> Lines of poetry (usually)

Proper nouns

> Names of people
> Geographical names
> Bodies of water
> Land features
> Streets, named buildings
> Specific places
> Ships, trains
> Brand names
> Nouns followed by a number or letter
> Companies, organizations
> Nationalities, races, religions
> Languages
> Gods or revered beings
> Events
> Holidays
> Titles of respect preceding a name

Proper adjectives

> Formed from proper nouns

Pronoun *I*

Have students discuss examples for each of the categories. Point out technicalities, such as the following:

1. Relationship terms are capitalized only if they are part of a person's name:

   Aunt Milly   my aunt
   Mother   their mother
   Cousin Brad   his cousin Brad

2. The directions north, south, east, and west are not capitalized unless they are specific or part of a name:

   North Winton Avenue   we turned north
   drove through the South   south of town

3. Common nouns used with proper adjectives are not capitalized:

   American government   Americans
   Venezuelan capital   African jungle

4. Short, unimportant words in a title are not capitalized; the first and last words are always capitalized:

   "Home, Home on the Range"
   Pardon Me, You're Stepping on my Eyeball!
   Where the Sidewalk Ends

5. Titles of books, films, plays, and any longer works are set in italics when printed (when typing or writing, we underline to indicate italics), thus:

   I am reading *Gone with the Wind.*
   We saw *Occurrence at Owl Creek Bridge* in our history class today.
   Miss Nelson Is Missing is a funny, funny book.
   (Note that *is* may be short, but it is important.)

Help students observe capitalization in literature. Discuss unusual uses of capitalization when they are noted in texts the students are reading. Plan occasional lessons that reinforce student knowledge of how to capitalize words according to contemporary conventions. *La dictée*[4] is a dictation strategy that reinforces knowledge of punctuation, capitalization, and spelling, as described in the following lesson.

A SAMPLE LESSON

TITLE: La Dictée, A Dictation Method

LEVEL: Grades 1–12 (Adapt materials selected.)

OBJECTIVES:

Students will:

1. Listen to sentences read aloud

2. Write each sentence dictated

3. Discuss spelling and mechanical errors

PROCEDURES:

Select a paragraph from a good book that students have already heard or one that you would like to introduce. Choose a paragraph that includes interesting sentence structures, varied uses of punctuation and capitalization, and new vocabulary. (Choose a less complex paragraph for the first experience with la dictée.) In this lesson we will use a paragraph from *Dragonwings* by Laurence Yep (Harper), a story of the Chinese in California during the early twenti th century.

Stimulus

Introduce the book and author to your class, for example:

> *Dragonwings* was written by a California author, Laurence Yep, who was inspired by the account of a Chinese immigrant who built a flying machine in 1909. This is how the story begins:
>
> "Ever since I can remember, I had wanted to know about the Land of the Golden Mountain, but my mother had never wanted to talk about it."

Invite students to conjecture about what the Land of the Golden Mountain is. Tell them that the main character, Moon Shadow, lives in China with his mother and grandmother, but his father, Wind-rider, lives in San Francisco's Chinatown.

Then share the interesting paragraph you have selected for the la dictée exercise, for example:

> Mother had talked quite a bit about him and so had Grand-mother; but that too was not the same. They were speaking about a young man who had lived in the Middle Kingdom, not a man who had endured the hardships and loneliness of living in the demon land. I knew he made kites; but as marvelous as his kites were, he and I could not spend the rest of our lives flying kites. I was afraid of the Golden Mountain, and yet my father, who lives there, wanted me to join him. I only knew that there was a certain rightness in life—the feeling you got when you did something the way you knew you should. I owed it to Father to obey him in everything—even if it meant going to such a fearful place as the Golden Mountain. And really, how really frightening could it be if Hand Clap wanted to go back? I turned to Mother and Grandmother. "I want to go," I said.

Talk about the passage the students have heard. Ask them such questions as:

1. Who is talking?

2. What characters are mentioned in this paragraph?

3. Who is Hand Clap?

4. What is this fearful place, The Golden Mountain? Where is it? How did it get that name?

5. Why was Moon Shadow afraid? Why did he decide to go?

Activity

Tell the students that you are going to dictate this paragraph to them, sentence by sentence. You will read each sentence only twice: The first time they are to listen without writing; the second time will be after they have begun writing. Challenge them to write each sentence as well as they can without help.

After you have completed the dictation exercise, have students correct any errors together. Ask two students to write the first sentence on the chalkboard. Ask if any changes need to be made in spelling, punctuation, or capitalization. Tell students to correct any mistakes they made on their own papers.

Follow-Up

Students should study this passage in preparation for writing the same passage again on the next day.

Evaluation

Have students compare the results of the two dictations. Have each one write several sentences summarizing what they learned from doing this exercise.

Have them staple the three papers together to place in their writing portfolios. Schedule la dictée lessons once a week for a period of time. After four weeks have each student examine his or her packet of dictation exercises to analyze how this learning experience is working, perhaps noting what he or she might do to improve performance on this task.

RELATED LEARNING ACTIVITIES

Extend student learning by providing instruction related to the literature you have introduced, as described in these examples.

1. *Repetition of the same dictation.* Dictate the same passage to students a month later to see if they have retained the knowledge. Students who have repeated difficulty can work together in pairs, dictating one sentence at a time to each other. This is a good exercise for ESL students.

2. *Exploring sentence patterns.* Choose a sentence from the passage to serve as a model for students. Show them how to identify the structural features of the sentence that form a pattern, thus:

_____ had _____
and so had _____ ; but that _____ .

Students can generate sentences that follow this pattern like this one:

John had lied and so had Mildred; but that didn't make any difference now.

3. *Responding to literature through writing.* This passage suggests a number of topics that seventh-grade students might identify, for example:

How would you feel if you were Moon Shadow? Would you have made the same decision?

Write the dialogue that you think might have taken place between Moon Shadow and his father, Windrider, when they met in San Francisco.

Each literature selection will suggest different ways of extending the learning of the students you work with. Follow-up activities may include dramatization, role playing, visualization, expanding and combining sentences, or character descriptions. Most students will be motivated to read the book that you introduce in this manner, so be sure to obtain a number of copies to share.

SUMMARY

Although we stress emphasizing the importance of the ideas expressed through student writing, we do need to teach students how to use the mechanics appropriately. These surface features can affect meaning, and they clearly do aid the reader in understanding what the writer is saying. The important thing is to teach the use of capitalization and punctuation through discovery methods so that students internalize the rationale for using these conventions as generally accepted. Lessons that guide students to observe how authors use the conventions in their writing will help students become aware that they can learn to write by reading.

Spelling

Spelling is very easy for some children who learn to spell conventionally as they learn to read. Without instruction they observe the patterns of words they encounter and are able to integrate them into their writing, as needed. These students don't require formal spelling instruction, at least as it is commonly presented.

In contrast, some very good readers don't seem to notice the patterns of letters that make up words they read. They grab the meaning of words without considering their physical makeup. This is fine in terms of comprehension, but it does leave students deficient in spelling ability. These students need instruction that focuses on visualizing the patterns that occur frequently and making connections between the sounds heard in spoken words and the combinations of letters we use to represent those sounds. Given this instruction, these students could potentially become good spellers, but it is important to help them in the early years.

A third group of students are poor readers for various reasons and, of course, they are also poor spellers. These students need instruction that emphasizes the close connections between reading and writing English. For example, using language experience methods with these students helps them recognize the connection between what they say and what they can read and write. They, too, need visualization practice and many writing experiences such as described in this section. Their reading and writing abilities will grow through integrated language arts activities.

We can help students with spelling difficulties in many ways, such as:

Review sound-symbol relationships (phonics)

Individualized techniques

Support during writing activities

Making connections during reading activities

Activities are described to help students with different aspects of spelling.

SOUND-SYMBOL RELATIONSHIPS

Linguists have identified approximately forty different sounds, called *phonemes*, that we use in speaking English words. We have at least one way of writing or spelling each of these sounds. Unfortunately, because our spelling system developed before we knew how the sound system (phonology) worked, we did not decide to spell each sound in one way so that there would never be any confusion; we do not have a one-to-one correspondence between sound and symbol. One reason we do not—actually, cannot—develop an easy spelling system is that we chose to use a twenty-six letter alphabet invented for another language when we wrote English. As we tried to spell forty sounds with twenty-six letters, we naturally ran into considerable difficulty.

The only rational way to show children and adults how to spell English is to begin with the sounds that we all learned to use at birth. Then we gradually introduce the ways of writing or spelling these sounds (graphemes) in English words. We begin with the easiest, most common, graphemes first. In the following examples, note that symbols written within slashes / / represent phonemes or sounds.

Common Sounds *(Phonemes)*	*Common Spellings* *(Graphemes)*
/b/	b as in baby
/t/	t as in toot
/p/	p as in pop

The consonants are heard more clearly because they are often the first sound in a word. We begin with the simplest sound-symbol correspondences, helping students hear the consonants at the beginning of words, even using words they might not have heard before. Thus, they learn to connect the beginning sounds and letters for words they want to spell.

Gradually, we introduce the idea that for some phonemes there are a number of alternate spellings. All of the twenty-four consonant sounds can be spelled in more than one way, and for some there are numerous alternate spellings. The common phoneme /f/, for instance, can be spelled *f* as in *fox* or *ph* as in *phone* or even *gh* as in *cough*.

The vowel sounds are more difficult than the consonants because all sixteen vowel phonemes have numerous alternate spellings or graphemes, as you will see in Table 5–1. We gradually introduce the more common vowel sounds and those that are most clearly heard.

This detailed chart is meant to provide background information for teachers. Even adult students will not find the chart helpful in improving their spelling. Students at any age need guidance in working their way through the simpler, more regular correspondences, into those that are less commonly used.

Again, we advocate using the discovery method. The methods described progress from easier ones, commonly used in primary grades, to those that are more advanced and might help older learners.

1. Say to the class: "The word *bird* begins with /b/." Write *bird* on the board and ask: "What other words begin like *bird?*" The class suggests words that begin with /b/:

blue	Bill	boo
balloon	book	bomb

   Place on the wall a picture of a bird with a large *b* printed on it. This will remind students of the correspondence between the sound they hear at the beginning of the word *bird* and the letter symbol they are learning to write. Students may clip pictures of *b* words to paste on a large sheet of paper. This exercise is repeated with other sound-symbol relationships. The knowledge is reinforced during language arts lessons whenever it occurs.

Table 5–1. Phoneme-Grapheme Chart

Consonants

Phonemes	Graphemes					
	Difficulty Level			*Examples*		
	1	*2*	*3*	*Initial*	*Medial*	*Final*
/b/	b			bill	tuber	cab
		bb			rubber	ebb
/d/	d			dill	coding	hard
		ed				pulled
		dd			sudden	Fudd
		ld				could
/f/	f			fill	fifer	loaf
		ph		phone	telephone	
		gh			roughing	cough
		ff			ruffle	off
			v			Chekhov
			pf (Ger.)	pfennig		
/g/	g			gill	tiger	bug
		gu		guest		
		gh		ghost		
		gg			logging	
			gue			catalogue
/h/	h			hill	unhappy	
		wh		who		
			j	José		
/j/	j			jam		
		g		giant	imagine	wage
		dg			judger	judge
			di		soldier	
			du		graduate	
			de		grandeur	
/k/	k			kill	raking	look
		ke				lake
		c		cat	act	
		qu (1)*		quit	equinox	
		qu (2)*			liquor	
		ck			lacking	pick

		cc			accost	
		x			fix	
			cu		biscuit	
			cch		bacchanal	
			ch	chorus		
			kh	khaki		
			cqu		acquit	
			que (1)		barbeque	
			que (2)			plaque
/l/	l			like	failing	fatal
		ll (1)**	ll (2)**	llama	calling	doll
/m/	m			mill	timer	ham
		me				come
		mm			simmer	
		mb			climbing	lamb
			mn			hymn
/n/	n			no	lining	fun
		ne				line
		kn		knot		
		gn		gnat		feign
		nn			runner	
			pn	pneumonia		
/p/	p			pill	caper	top
		pp			copper	Lapp
/r/	r			rose	caring	fair
		rr			carry	Carr
		wr		write		
			rh	rhyme		
/s/	s			so		thus
		c		cell	receive	
		sc		scent		
		ss			classes	toss
		x				fox
			ps	pseudo		
/t/	t			to	later	hit
		tt			hotter	mutt
		bt			debtor	debt
		ed				licked

Table 5–1. (*continued*)

Consonants

Phonemes	Graphemes					
	Difficulty Level			*Examples*		
	1	*2*	*3*	*Initial*	*Medial*	*Final*
			pt	ptomaine		receipt
			dt			veldt
			th	Thomas		
/v/	v			very	cover	
		f				of
		ve				weave
			ph		Stephen	
			vv		flivver	
/w/	w			will	slower	how
		one		one		
		wh		while	awhile	
			qu (kw)		quit	
			ui		suite	
			oui	ouija		
/y/	y			yes	lawyer	
			j		hallelujah	
			io		onion	
			ll		bouillon	
/z/	z			zoo	dozing	whiz
		s(e)			miser	lose, is
		zz			dazzle	buzz
		ss			Missouri	
			sc		discern	
			x	xylophone		
			cz	czar		
/č/	ch			child		much
		tch			matches	hutch
			c	cello		
			cz	Czech		
			eou		righteous	
			t		nature	
/š/	sh			shoe	worship	rush

	s		sugar		
	ch		champagne		
		sch	schist		
		ce		ocean	
		si		mansion	
		ss		mission	
		sci		luscious	
		ti		patient	
		xi		anxious	
		chs		fuchsia	
/ž/	g		gendarme (Fr)	adagio	garage
	s (i)			pleasure, Asia	
	z (i)			brazier	
		j	jejeune		
/θ/	th		thimble	ether	loathe
/ð/	th		the	either	breath
/ŋ/	ng			ringer	wing
	nk			think	
		ngue			tongue

Diphthongs

Phonemes	Graphemes
/iy/ (long e)	see, sea, me, deceive, believe, carbine, ski, gladly, Aesop, people, quay, key, suite, equator, Phoenix
/ey/ (long a)	bay, rain, gate, they, gauge, break, neigh, rein, straight, care
/ay/ (long i)	kite, right, I, by, cries, find, buy, height, eye, stein, aisle, dye, aye, lyre, iodine
/ow/ (long o)	lone, road, foe, slow, dough, beau, sew, yeoman, whoa, odor, oh, solo, soul, brooch
/yuw/ (long u)	use, few, view, beautiful, queue
/oy/	toy, moist
/aw/	now, out, bough
/uw/	too, blew, tune, suit, lose, flu, do, canoe, though, tomb, blue, group, prove, maneuver

Simple Vowels

Phonemes	Graphemes	
/i/	give, pit, myth, quilt, busy, women, England, sieve, been	
/e/	red, said, breath, friend, any, leopard (leisure), says, aesthetics, their, foetid	
/æ/	had, have, laugh, plaid	Unaccented Syllables
/ə/	nut, flood, rough, son, of, dove, was, does	cattle ahead fountain parliament
/a/	ah, halt, hot, mirage, cart, heart, fault, sergeant	moment happily burgeon porpoise
/u/	good, full, put, wolf, could	
/ɔ/	caught, jaw, talk, fought, daughter, watch, broad, toss, otter, Utah	
/ɨ/	her, sir, fur, work, satyr, journey, heard, grammar	

* In the initial position the grapheme qu (1) spells the blended phonemes /kw/; in other positions qu (2) is usually an alternate spelling for /k/.
** The grapheme ll (2) is very rare in the initial position. For that reason it is considered a difficult spelling while the ll (1) grapheme is rather common.
Source: Iris M. Tiedt, *The Language Arts Handbook,* © 1983, Prentice Hall, pp. 208–212. Reprinted by permission of Prentice Hall, Inc., Englewood Cliffs, New Jersey.

2. Individualized spelling dictionaries help students of all ages as they record words they use often but consistently have trouble with. Students can test each other periodically to see if they know how to spell any words which they can then remove from their dictionaries. These words come directly from student writing experiences.

3. Word Walls are brainstormed in a classroom as students prepare to write about a given topic, for instance, Halloween. The teacher writes the words as students suggest them. Thus, they have ready assistance with spelling words they need to use in writing; the words also suggest ideas.

4. A Spelling Demon Chart posted in the classroom helps students with words that most people find tricky. Students can

be challenged to see if they can pass the Spelling Demon Test given periodically by the teacher or a student who has passed the test. A class may choose to add words to this standard list.

5. Spelling games add to the fun of working with language, removing some of the tedium of having to learn to spell. This poem about English spelling makes a point but also requires the students to know the alternate spellings involved.

> You don't spell penny
> The way you spell any.
>
> The ending of nickel
> Is different than pickle.
>
> You cannot spell bun
> The way you spell won.
>
> You wrestle with busy
> Until you are dizzy.
>
> It makes your head hurt
> To try to spell dirt.
>
> Let me tell you, honey,
> Spelling can be funny.

Students will also enjoy working with codes which require knowledge of spelling, for example:

A = 1	J = 10	S = 19
B = 2	K = 11	T = 20
C = 3	L = 12	U = 21
D = 4	M = 13	V = 22
E = 5	N = 14	W = 23
F = 6	O = 15	X = 24
G = 7	P = 16	Y = 25
H = 8	Q = 17	Z = 26
I = 9	R = 18	

As you can see, students at all levels need support in identifying appropriate spellings for the words they know how to say. Gradually, however, through listening, speaking, thinking, reading, and writing the English language, they do learn how to manage the complexities of the spelling system. For most adults, spelling is a continuous learning experience as we venture into writing words borrowed from other languages or deal with such perpetual demons as *grammar, accommodate,* and *receive.*

SUMMARY

Spelling instruction is part of composition instruction; the only reason to know how to spell is to be able to communicate through writing. In this context, spelling is a complex of conventions agreed upon by writers of English that have been recorded in dictionaries. Typically, spelling is taught as a subject separate from other subjects. Little effort has been made to teach students the interrelationships among spoken English and spelling or the connections between reading (phonics) and spelling. Spelling instruction has been greatly overemphasized, particularly in the elementary school, in terms of time spent on instruction and success rate. We do need to help students spell English words accurately because spelling has value in our society. Methods should emphasize both visual and auditory approaches to learning that focus on patterns of spelling and the sound-symbol relationships. Learning to spell should be an individualized matter taught within the context of writing instruction.

Form

The primary focus in writing should be on ideas. Attention to form, however, does play a part in communicating these ideas effectively in writing.

We can think of form in two different ways. All writing is presented in some form, for example, a list, a song, an essay, a sonnet, and so on. Therefore, students need to have some knowledge of varied forms of writing—the features of specific forms they will try to write. We also are aware of the form or format of a paper, that is, its physical appearance. As students edit their work to a final presentation, they need to consider practices of indentation, legibility, and the concept of "clean copy." These topics fit appropriately in a discussion of the conventions of writing.

Varied Forms of Writing

Students come to school knowing a number of forms of writing: notes posted on the refrigerator door, grocery lists, birthday cards, letters from grandmother, and stories. Of particular interest is the child's "sense of story" that begins developing at birth. We tell stories, sharing ourselves, throughout our lives. Storytelling is part of being human.

As students encounter literature, whether read aloud to them or read independently, they become aware of other forms. They come to identify various types of stories as well as other types of prose—newspaper articles, letters to the editor, editorials, informative nonfiction, essays, and so on. They also meet poetry, beginning with Mother Goose and jump rope jingles and progressing to the more sophisticated writing of Robert Frost, Carl Sandburg, or Langston Hughes.

We can plan instruction that will assist students in clarifying their knowledge of the forms that writing can take. We can help them discover the characteristics of each of these various forms. In the following lesson plan, students discover the distinctive features of a narrative form, the fable.

SAMPLE LESSON

TITLE: The Features of a Fable

LEVEL: Grades 3–12

OBJECTIVES:

Students will:

1. Listen to several fables

2. Identify the distinctive features of a fable

3. Generate a list of proverbs

4. Write an original fable

PROCEDURES:

Collect several examples of fables. The classic fables by Aesop are good short examples suitable for any grade level. You might also look for modern fables, for example: *Fables* by Arnold Lobel, *Once a Mouse . . . A Fable Cut in Wood* by Marcia Brown, or *Fables for Our Time* by James Thurber. You may wish to place this Aesop fable on an overhead transparency for presentation to the class.

> *The Ant and the Grasshopper*
>
> In a field one summer's day a grasshopper was hopping about, chirping and singing to its heart's content. An ant passed by, bearing along with great toil an ear of corn he was taking to the nest.
>
> "Why not come and chat with me," said the grasshopper, "instead of toiling and moiling in that way?"
>
> "I am helping to lay up food for the winter," said the ant, "and I recommend that you do the same."
>
> "Why bother about winter?" said the grasshopper. "We have plenty of food at present."
>
> But the ant went on its way and continued its toil. When the winter came the grasshopper had no food, and found itself dying of hunger, while it saw the ants distributing every day corn and grain from the stores they had collected in the summer. Then the grasshopper knew—
>
> *It is best to prepare for the days of necessity.*
>
> Retold by Joseph Jacobs in *The Fables of Aesop* (Macmillan, 1894).

Stimulus

Read several fables aloud to the class. Ask students what kind of writing this is (narrative, story). Elicit (or supply) the term *fable*.

Then invite students to suggest the characteristics of a fable that they have observed in the stories you read. You may wish to display a short fable on an overhead projector. Write the suggested features on the board, thus:

Features of a Fable

1. Has animal characters.

2. Animals behave like humans. They talk and have human traits, for example, greed or jealousy.

3. Tells a story; has plot structure.

4. Ends with a moral, a proverb, or a wise saying; teaches a lesson.

5. Conflict between good and evil; good triumphs.

If students miss one or more of these ideas, you may question them to be sure these main ideas are covered.

Guide students to observe that the moral is a proverb or wise saying. Ask them if they know other similar wise sayings. Brainstorm a list of proverbs (asking two students to record them as they are suggested), for example:

A stitch in time saves nine.

Look before you leap.

Don't cry over spilt milk.

He who laughs last laughs best.

Too many cooks spoil the broth.

A fool and his money are soon parted.

A bird in the hand is worth two in the bush.

Activity

Have the students work in pairs to create a fable that illustrates one of the given proverbs (or another one that occurs to them). Have students refer to the Features List on the board. Each dyad should choose two animal characters, deciding what characteristics they will have; one character will be good while the other is evil. Then they can choose a proverb for the moral of their fable. The setting, dialogue, and plot development should then create a situation in which the events will lead to that conclusion.

Follow-Up

Have students read their fables aloud to the whole group. The class might make evaluative comments about what they like best about each fable after it is read.

Students should revise their fables based on the comments made about all of the fables and other ideas they may have gained by listening to the fables written by their classmates. Each fable should be printed neatly, perhaps illustrated, for inclusion in a class book of Fable Fun.

Evaluation

Observe student participation during brainstorming sessions and during the team writing activity.

Listen to the fables to see that students understand the features identified and have been able to include them in writing. Have students write fables individually as homework. They should read them in response groups of four or five students to revise their work appropriately. These fables can then be added to the class book.

Illustrated in this lesson is one effective way of guiding students to clarify their knowledge about a specific form of writing. Similar lessons can be presented focusing on the fairy tale, a report of information, or a biographical sketch. Lessons presented elsewhere in this book also utilize this discovery or inquiry method which engages students in developing thinking skills as they also learn to write.

FORMAT

Students need to become aware of conventions about presenting their writing on paper. One basic convention that is sometimes confusing is indentation.

We follow certain basic rules about indenting, for example: The first word in a paragraph is indented. Students sometimes generalize from this rule that indentation, therefore, signals a new paragraph. They may use indenting as a synonym for "paragraphing." Therein lies confusion.

As soon as you examine a passage of dialogue, for instance, you see that indentation is used also to signal a change of speaker, thus:

> "Oh," she cried. "I'm afraid I can't help you work in the garden today."
> Mrs. Roberts smiled at her friend. "That's all right," she remarked. "I think I can manage quite nicely."

We must be careful to distinguish between indenting to separate one developed paragraph from another and indenting to distinguish the speech of one person from another. Narrative prose requires the use of indentation for both purposes. The short speeches include above are, of course, not developed paragraphs. Although indented, they should not be called paragraphs. We should drop the term *paragraphing* and use *indenting* instead.

Conventions for indenting are also followed when presenting long quoted passages. The long quotation is indented twice, as shown here, and students should observe that these quotations do not require quotation marks because indentation sets them apart.

> For too long the classroom was a silent place in which children were "to be seen and not heard." Studies show that children are literally afraid to ask questions in school. Why would this be true when young children are so full of questions as they go busily about their work of discovering the world? We need to consider how we can correct this attitude, for children learn by questioning.[5]

SUMMARY

Although we make it clear to students that the most important thing about writing is the thinking they express—the ideas—students do need to become aware of form in writing. We can guide them to discover a variety of forms that writing can take in both poetry and prose, fiction and nonfiction. We also help students deal with the conventions of formatting writing on the page and using different ways of indenting words as markers, which convey meaning to the reader much as punctuation does.

Proofreading

As discussed earlier, proofreading is the final process before a piece of writing is published (made public). Proofreading is not the same as editing, which is a much broader term that includes the full revision process from first draft to publication. Editing includes proofreading.

The final duty of a writer is to proofread the printed copy of his or her writing. Marking the printed proof for the printer, indicating changes to be made before publication, the author returns the proof to the printer as quickly as possible so as not to delay the publishing process.

Student writers also need to reread the final copy of their writing to be sure no errors have slipped in accidentally. We can recommend that students use such techniques as these:

1. Read the manuscript backwards. Beginning with the last word, the writer reads word by word to observe spelling carefully.

2. Exchange papers with another student. Read each other's paper aloud slowly to determine that no words have been left out and to note any questionable spellings.

3. Mark another student's paper with printer's proofreading marks (which can be found in most dictionaries) to indicate corrections that should be made.

Reflection

When students are composing any piece of writing, their focus should be on presenting sound, interesting ideas. Worrying about mechanics, spelling, and other conventions of writing should be set aside until the ideas are roughed out. When students are ready to make their writing public, however, they do need to consider the person who will read it. They need to add appropriate punctuation marks and to use conventional spelling, making every effort to present their writing in the best light possible. Working together in peer groups, they will assist each other through the full editing process: writing the rough draft, revising, and, finally, proofreading the manuscript. Preparing a fully edited clean copy for publication reveals pride in what the student has produced.

Challenge

Try these ideas as you prepare for teaching the conventions with a group of students.

1. Make a large chart of selected proofreader's marks that you think your students might benefit from using as they edit each other's writing.

2. Select a book from Chapter 8 that you would like to read aloud to your students. As you preview the book, note the following:

   a. A good passage for presenting through the "la dictée" strategy.

   b. One or more pages that illustrate the use of quotation marks in dialogue.

   c. Other passages that illustrate the use of specific punctuation or capitalization conventions.

3. Review the phoneme-grapheme chart in this chapter. Plan a series of lessons based on this information that would be useful in helping your students learn to spell accurately.

Endnotes

1. Charlton Laird. *A Writer's Handbook*. Lexington, MA: Ginn, 1964, p. 358.

2. Edgar Schuster. "Let's Get Off the Mythmobile." *English Journal* (October 1985): 40–41.

3. Iris M. Tiedt. *The Language Arts Handbook*. Englewood Cliffs, NJ: Prentice-Hall, 1983, p. 197.

4. Iris M. Tiedt. "La Dictée: An Effective Method for Teaching Writing." ERIC, 1984.

5. Iris M. Tiedt. *Exploring Books with Children*. Boston: Houghton Mifflin, 1979, p. 344.

Exploring Further

Geuder, Patricia et al. *They Really Taught Us How to Write*. ERIC, 1974.

Harris, Muriel. *Teaching One-to-One*. National Council of Teachers of English, 1986.

Hodges, John C., and Whitten, Mary E. *Harbrace College Handbook*. Harcourt, 1986.

Mathews, Dorothy, ed. *Writing Assignments Based on Literary Works*. Illinois English Bulletin, Spring 1985.

Tiedt, Iris M. *The Language Arts Handbook*. Prentice-Hall, 1983.

Tiedt, Iris M. et al. *Teaching Writing in K-8 Classrooms*. Prentice-Hall, 1983.

6

Evaluating
Student Writing

I am convinced more and more every day that fine writing is, next to fine doing, the top thing in the world.

John Keats

The positive stance advocated in this book demands that evaluation of student writing emphasize the worth of each student's efforts. Thus, our focus in this chapter is on communicating that worth directly to students and also to their parents. This approach involves the students themselves in assessing the value of their writing and the measure of their progress. We are concerned here with evaluation that is individualized, designed to promote learning. Perhaps it is idealistic, but we would hope, too, that more and more students might share the feelings of Keats, above, that writing is a fine thing to be doing.

As has been noted elsewhere, evaluation and editing of student writing are closely related. As students meet in editing groups to share their writing for the purpose of improving and developing it, evaluation of what has been written necessarily takes place. Evaluation at this formative stage is more helpful in terms of student learning than summative evaluation of a completed manuscript. For this reason, formative evaluation should be included in writing workshop plans almost every day.

We are, of course, interested in determining the most effective methods of assessing student writing abilities both for the purpose of informing the individual about his or her writing competency and for informing the district about the effectiveness of writing instruction. The same methods may be used for both purposes. We will examine holistic, analytical, and primary trait methods, noting the characteristics of each and how each method can be used to best advantage.

After reading this chapter, you should be able to:

1. Explain the importance of involving students in evaluation of their own writing

2. Suggest ways of engaging students in evaluating each other's writing

3. Define the characteristics of holistic, analytic, and primary trait types of assessment

4. Compare alternative methods for recording progress of individual students

Looking at Evaluation Practices

Evaluation of student writing has long been a problem for the classroom teacher. Through the years K–12 teachers somehow internalized the expectation that good teachers of writing read every piece of writing their students generate and that they correct every error these students make. This expectation proved to be overwhelming—so overwhelming that teachers avoided having their students write, because grading all of those papers was just too much work. Fortunately, thinking has changed over the past decade, and none too soon.

Research and teacher experience have shown us methods of teaching writing that are not only wiser, but more effective and more enjoyable. We now are spreading the word to teachers across the grades, letting them know that:

1. Students should write every day, but teachers should not expect to read everything their students write.

2. The emphasis should be on ideas, not error avoidance, and teachers should not serve as copy editors for their students.

3. Students learn to write best through editing and evaluating their own writing and that of their peers.

With the paperload removed from their shoulders, teachers can have their students write more frequently. Teachers can use their expertise to plan exciting writing activities. They can guide their students to edit and to evaluate their own writing and that of their peers.

PURPOSES OF EVALUATION

Why spend time on evaluating student writing? This question might well be posed to the students in your class, generating discussion of such considerations as:

1. What does evaluation mean?

2. How is evaluation done and by whom?

3. Are there different ways of evaluating writing?

4. What are the purposes of evaluation?

Evaluation or assessment of student writing requires considerable time, which can be equated in monetary terms. Unless the purpose and the outcomes make it worthwhile, the cost in time and money may outweigh the value. We need to look at the purposes for evaluation carefully.

One major purpose for evaluating student writing is to inform the writer and his or her parents and teachers just how this writer is performing or what he or she knows about writing. Evaluation of student writing assesses an individual student's writing ability at one point in time. This assessment can then be compared to a sampling assessed at an earlier time to reveal a student's progress. This assessment can also be compared to the performance of other students writing on the same topic in a similar testing situation.

Another purpose for evaluating writing is to inform schools, districts, or whole states how well students are writing at different levels. The performance of the student writers may also reveal something about the quality of instruction. Poor student performance may indicate the need for staff development on teaching writing.

Evaluation of writing in the classroom informs individual students about the quality of their writing at any stage of development. Formative evaluation thereby guides the young writer in revising a manuscript or deciding on alternative ways of developing and presenting the ideas he or she is considering. Thus, evaluation and editing processes are integral, related aspects of composition.

All of these purposes for evaluation are valid. All will be used at different times during a school year. Obviously, the latter purpose will be practiced regularly within the individual classroom as a part of the writing program. Certainly one of our instructional objectives should be to teach students the value of evaluation and to remove the apprehension from evaluation experiences.

WRITING SAMPLE VERSUS OBJECTIVE TESTS

In the past, writing ability was largely assessed by asking students questions *about* writing, their knowledge of grammar and usage. Students were asked to select from multiple choices the best written sentence or to identify writing that contained a grammatical error. This type of test, with answers recorded on an answer sheet, was quickly scored for large numbers of students.

This indirect method of evaluating a student's writing was attacked by teachers who argued that knowing *about* writing was not the same as performing writing. Teachers across the country pleaded for the direct assessment of student writing. The obstacle to evaluating student writing samples was, of course, the enormity of the scoring task. Holistic scoring techniques were developed that made it possible to score thousands of student papers in one day. Thus began the movement toward improved writing instruction which included holistic assessment.

Today, methods of scoring student writing samples are being perfected. The Educational Testing Service, working with the California State Department of Education, has devised a matrix scoring technique to score some 300,000 eighth-grade writing samples in

1987. This matrix includes elements drawn from analytic scoring of the use of conventions, holistic scoring of student ability to write various types of writing, and evaluation of primary traits of good writing.

USES OF WRITING TESTS

"Writing is a multi-dimensional skill of such complexity that no one-number score can describe it accurately," notes Richard Stiggins, speaking for the Northwest Regional Educational Laboratory. He observes that we need to be aware of the present evaluation methods but also be prepared for the development of alternative methods. The Northwest Regional Educational Laboratory has identified eight different uses for writing test scores and the assessment methods that seem to be consistent with each use.

Test Context	Type of Scoring		
	Holistic	*Analytic*	*Primary Trait*
1. Instruction Management			
a. Diagnosis		x	x
b. Placement	x	x	x
c. Guidance	x	x	x
2. Student Screening			
a. Selection	x	?	?
b. Certification of minimal competencies		x	x
3. Program Evaluation			
a. Survey evaluation	x		
b. Formative evaluation	x	x	x
c. Summative evaluation	x	x	x

Stiggins also states that studies of commercial tests available today show that they do tend to include at least an optional writing sample. In 1979–81, 58 percent of new tests included an optional writing sample compared to 0 percent in tests of 1973–75.[1]

IDENTIFYING THE FEATURES OF GOOD WRITING

One of the side benefits that has come from efforts to assess student writing more accurately is the identification of the features of good writing. Teachers are now talking about the characteristics of effective writing among themselves. They have created rubrics, criteria for judging student writing, based on what they themselves know about writing.

What is even more exciting is that they have begun talking with students about the quality indicators of good writing. Teachers are inviting students from all grade levels to make lists of what kinds of things a good writer does and what features good writing contains. Writing, of course, improves as teachers guide students to include these qualities of effective writing in their own writing.

This list was compiled by a class of third graders who had talked about the qualities of good writing with their teacher.

A good writer:

Begins sentences with capital letters.

Ends sentences with a period or question mark.

Uses interesting words.

Paints a picture we can see.

Finds out how to spell words he or she needs to write.

Tells a good story with a beginning, middle, and an end.

The following list was compiled by a group of teachers attending a summer writing institute.

A good writer:

Conventions

    Writes grammatical sentences
    Spells so misspelling doesn't detract
    Uses or invents punctuation conventions to aid the reader
    Writes legibly or types

Creativity, Style

> Uses descriptive language and imagery
> Chooses varied vocabulary
> Uses words precisely
> Has original ideas and ways of expressing them
> Uses varied types and lengths of sentences
> Uses rhythm and flow of language
> Hooks or grabs reader's attention
> Tries the unexpected and takes risks
> Adjusts style to purpose and audience
> Communicates feelings and emotions
> Includes sensory imagery and assists visualization
> Chooses active verbs rather than passive

Organization

> Supports statements with evidence
> Develops topic fully
> Uses varied genres or types of writing
> Displays clear structure in writing
> Employs logical thinking

Process

> Has a knowledge base and accurate data
> Focuses and selects what is appropriate
> Revises and proofreads writing

These lists represent the knowledge of the group that compiled them. Each list will grow as the group gains new information about the writing process.

Direct Methods of Assessing Writing Performance

In this section we will address direct methods of assessing student performance that are in use across the country. These methods include analytic, holistic, and primary trait assessment. We will examine the intent and procedures for each. In the final section we will discuss how these assessment procedures fit into classroom instruction.

ANALYTIC ASSESSMENT

Analytic evaluation is detailed analysis usually based on a scale or checklist. The scale is "a list of the prominent features or characteristics of a piece of writing."[2] The features selected for evaluation vary according to the context of the specific writing assignment, the audience, and the purpose for writing.

Analytic assessment of writing has value, but there are inherent dangers. A detailed analysis of student writing is time consuming, and it does tend to emphasize error analysis. It is the kind of thing that teachers did regularly for many years as they corrected the errors on student papers and wrote helpful suggestions in the margins. Analytic assessment can, of course, be positive, noting all of the many accomplishments of the writer, but somehow we forget to take that approach to evaluating student writing. The kinds of errors commonly checked include the mechanics, spelling, grammar, and usage—surface features. Instruction based on analytic assessment tends to stress error avoidance, which, as we have noted, should not be our primary concern in teaching writing.

Following is an analytical checklist that attempts to assess general knowledge of the conventions of writing but also includes aspects of creativity and form. This checklist could be effectively used in assessing narrative writing, perhaps the writing of a short story.

The Tiedt Analytical Checklist for Composition

A method of analyzing errors and assessing creative elements of writing to guide instruction.

	Strong 5	Average 3	Weak 1	Count
A. FLUENCY (ease; length)	___	___	___	
1. Number of words				___
2. Number of sentences				___
B. FLEXIBILITY (variety)	___	___	___	

	Strong 5	Average 3	Weak 1	Count
1. Number of t-units (subj/pred)				_____
2. Average t-unit length				_____
3. Complex sentences (beyond kernel)				_____
C. ELABORATION (detail)	_____	_____	_____	
1. Adjective/ Adjectivals				_____
2. Adverb/Adverbials				_____
3. Figures of speech				_____
			Total 1	_____
D. ORIGINALITY (uniqueness)	_____	_____	_____	
1. Imagery	_____	_____	_____	
2. Interest quality	_____	_____	_____	
3. Humor	_____	_____	_____	
E. FORM (structure)	_____	_____	_____	
1. Organization clear	_____	_____	_____	
2. Indentation	_____	_____	_____	
3. Title	_____	_____	_____	
4. Handwriting	_____	_____	_____	
F. CONVENTIONS				Error No.
1. Spelling	_____	_____	_____	_____
2. Punctuation	_____	_____	_____	_____
3. Capitalization	_____	_____	_____	_____
4. Usage (word choice)	_____	_____	_____	_____
5. Grammar (syntax)	_____	_____	_____	_____
Total scores 3	_____	_____	_____ 2	_____

Individual Student Summary   Class Rank

Total 1	_____	(Creative Elements)	_____
Total 2	_____	(Convention Errors) Invert	_____
Total 3	_____	(Overall Writing Ability)	_____

Source: Adapted from Iris M. Tiedt, *The Language Arts Handbook*, © 1983, Prentice Hall, pp. 176–177. Prentice Hall, Inc., Englewood Cliffs, New Jersey.

Begins sentences with capital letters.

Using this scale gives the teacher a score for creative elements in a student's writing, a score for convention errors, and an overall score of writing ability that includes creative and organizational skills. Student scores are ranked within a class or grade level for purposes of comparison. Note that the best score for errors is low, whereas the other two scores would be high. In ranking the error scores, we can invert the order accordingly.

Following is a second checklist that is more appropriate for assessing expository prose. It categorizes the analysis into content, organization, vocabulary, and mechanics:

Writing Assessment

	Strength	*Weakness*
CONTENT		
Develops the topic		
*details	_____	_____
*examples	_____	_____
*reasons	_____	_____
Ingenuity, creativity, originality	_____	_____
Individual style	_____	_____
ORGANIZATION		
Clear plan of organization		
*beginning	_____	_____
*middle	_____	_____
*end	_____	_____
Addresses all sections of prompt	_____	_____
Stays on the topic	_____	_____
Maintains order	_____	_____
Clear transitions	_____	_____
VOCABULARY		
Precise word choice	_____	_____
Clear, accurate usage	_____	_____
Vivid, concrete language	_____	_____
MECHANICS		
Sentence structure		

	Strength	Weakness
*complete sentences	_____	_____
*clear, logical sentences	_____	_____
*variety of sentence structure	_____	_____
Paragraphing	_____	_____
Punctuation		
*appropriate end punctuation	_____	_____
*dialogue punctuation	_____	_____
*internal punctuation	_____	_____
Spelling	_____	_____
Usage		
*pronoun forms	_____	_____
*verb forms	_____	_____
Other		
_____	_____	_____
_____	_____	_____
_____	_____	_____

Source: Tiedt/Bruemmer/Lane/Stelwagon/Watanabe/Williams, *Teaching Writing in K–8 Classrooms: The Time Has Come,* © 1983, Prentice Hall, p. 226. Reprinted by permission of Prentice Hall, Inc., Englewood Cliffs, New Jersey.

The chief value of a detailed analysis is to guide instruction. For this purpose, the more detailed the analysis the better. The teacher can plan instruction for those students who are clearly having difficulty with quotation marks or those who need to work on vocabulary development. If few students are including imagery in their writing, class lessons should focus on recognizing similes and metaphors in writing that you read aloud. You may wish to take notes about specific problems students have as you analyze a class set of papers following one of these checklists.

Used occasionally in combination with holistic assessment, the analytic assessment benefits the individual learner. For purposes of general assessment of writing achievement across a large population, however, we seldom need to be so precise in assessing writing. The holistic assessment answers the need for a quick, less expensive method of assessment.

HOLISTIC ASSESSMENT

The word *holistic* comes from the same Greek root as our English word *whole*. If we look at something holistically, we look at the whole thing, with little attempt to analyze specific features. Holistic evaluation is defined as "a guided procedure for sorting or ranking written pieces."[3] A reader ranks a sample of student writing by:

1. Matching it with another piece in a graded series of pieces

2. Scoring it for the prominence of certain features important to that kind of writing

3. Assigning it a letter or number grade.[4]

Holistic scoring is used for large-scale assessment because it is quick. The reader reads a sample rapidly, getting an overall impression of quality. Usually a set of criteria guides readers in their general assessment, but the criteria are quickly internalized so that referral to the criteria (called a rubric) is necessary only in cases of doubt.

As someone has said, "The whole is greater than the sum of its parts." The intent of holistic assessment is to provide a score that indicates the general quality of a student's writing as a whole with no attempt to analyze specific errors. Although some have criticized this method of evaluating student writing, researchers find a high degree of reliability among scorers using the techniques recommended. Holistic scoring has been widely used and tested across the country.[5]

Holistic assessment follows well-defined requirements that have been formalized through repeated applications of the method. The procedures require the following:

1. Selection of a topic or prompt

2. Establishment of criteria (rubric) for scoring

3. Administration of the writing sample

4. Scoring

5. Report of results

Selecting a Topic

The selection of a prompt or topic on which all students will write is crucial. The topic must be sufficiently general so that all students will have knowledge and experience from which to discuss the topic. At the same time, we want students to write about something that is interesting—a topic they will be motivated to respond to in detail. It is not uncommon for topics to prove less successful than teachers would have predicted. Two topics that have been widely used, and tested for success with large numbers of students, are the following:

- If you were to become an animal, what animal would you choose? Write a story for your classmates that tells why you chose to be that animal and what life is like as that animal. You may write from the point of view of the animal, assuming that it can talk and has human traits.

- Describe an object that means a lot to you. You might explain how you got the object, what it means to you, and how it has become important to you over the years.

Notice that the prompt usually leads students to write a specific type of writing. If we want students to write narrative prose, then we should ask students to tell a story, as in the first example. The words *describe* and *explain* in the second prompt will probably lead students to write expository prose.

Once the prompt has been selected, then teachers should try writing to the topic. In this way they anticipate problems students will have in responding to this prompt. Teachers will then be better able to establish the criteria for evaluating student writing, which is the next task to be accomplished.

Establishing Criteria for Successful Writing

Teachers have always been accustomed to reading student papers and dropping them into piles—perhaps, only three at first: outstanding work, average work, and very weak work. Conscious of the need to supply grades, usually the traditional A–F, we then sort through the largest pile of average papers to decide which ones deserve a plus and could legitimately get a B, and which ones are decidedly weaker and deserve a grade of D. As we sorted the papers, we operated according to an internalized perception of what good work is. We all have these notions of what it takes to get an A on a paper, but we seldom put our ideas on paper, and we almost never communicate them clearly to our students.

One of the major contributions of holistic assessment is the clarification of these criteria for evaluating student writing. Holistic scoring includes the creation of rubrics, a clear delineation of the features of writing for each of the scores specified. For the first time, teachers sat down together to talk about the qualities of good writing. Observe the specific features of the writing students are expected to produce for each of the scoring levels in the following rubrics.

A Sample for Grades 1–8: Expository Writing

Score	Characteristics
5	Writes at least one coherent paragraph on given topic Includes details, interesting words Uses varied sentence structures Relatively free from error Uses transitional devices Demonstrates some originality of expression
3	Writes an organized paragraph Sticks to the topic Uses some descriptive words Makes some mechanical or spelling errors
1	Writes one sentence or more Shows little evidence of paragraph construction Makes numerous mechanical and spelling errors
0	Writes little or nothing Writes on a different topic

South Bay Writing Project
Holistic Scoring Materials: Rubric

Score	*Criteria for Score*

0   No writing submitted.

1   The writer lacks understanding of the topic.
   a. fails to communicate with the reader
   b. confused sense of audience
   c. general lack of coherence or evidence of purpose
   d. generally weak grasp of spelling, punctuation, syntax
   e. no sense of paragraph development

3   The writer understands the topic and writes relatively clearly.
   a. lacks singleness of purpose
   b. contains some irrelevancies
   c. shows some attempt at organizing material coherently
   d. some attempt at paragraph development
   e. some knowledge of spelling, punctuation, syntax
   f. paper still marked by frequent errors

5   The writer presents fairly competent discussion of the topic.
   a. uses examples and/or details
   b. purpose reasonably clear
   c. evidence of adequate organization with few irrelevancies
   d. paragraphing is generally competent
   e. clear sense of conclusion
   f. mechanical errors do not interfere with meaning
   g. syntax generally adequate

7   The writer presents full discussion of topic with well-chosen examples and details for support.
   a. reveals some elaboration and refinement of ideas
   b. well-organized with clear beginning, middle, and end

South Bay Writing Project
Holistic Scoring Materials: Rubric (*continued*)

Score	*Criteria for Score*

      c. clear sense of purpose and audience
      d. generally competent mechanically
      e. few run-ons or fragments; good sense of syntax
      f. variety of sentence structures

9   The writer presents an unusually complete and/or imaginative development of the topic.
      a. striking use of evidence, examples, details
      b. outstanding organization with effective opening and conclusion
      c. evidence of reasoning
      d. clear sense of writer control of voice, purpose, audience
      e. correct, mature, varied sense of sentence structure
      f. free of mechanical errors

Agreeing on the criteria for judging the quality of student writing prepares the teachers to begin scoring the district writing sample. First, however, we need to collect the writing sample from the group of students to be evaluated.

Administering the Writing Test

Teachers need to agree on procedures for administering the writing test. They also need to agree on just how the writing assignment will be presented to the students and appropriate behaviors for teachers involved. Alternatives can be considered for the following questions with a vote deciding how all will conduct the writing sample:

1. Should students know the topic on which they will write so they can prepare at least a day ahead for the writing test? (Usually students are not given the topic (prompt) in advance.)

2. Will students have a prewriting warm-up discussion about the prompt? (Teachers usually decide to talk about ideas for about ten minutes before students begin to write.)

3. Can students use dictionaries or other tools? (Opinions vary, but using dictionaries does focus on error avoidance and does slow down student writing.)

Teachers should discuss any problems they foresee and make appropriate decisions before administering the test. Every effort should be made to have all teachers administer the writing test in the same way so that realistic comparisons can be made. A sample Direction Sheet is provided as part of the training material presented in Chapter 7.

Agree on a date for administering the test in each elementary classroom or in each English classroom. Teachers should collect student papers and turn them into the central office immediately so that there is no opportunity for their being altered in any way.

Students who are absent on the day of the examination can meet at the beginning of the next day in the library to write the first thing in the morning. As soon as the writing sample has been collected, the papers are ready for scoring.

Holistic Scoring of Papers

Even the most experienced of teachers need training each time they prepare for the holistic scoring of student writing. Someone must serve as the coordinator of the training sessions. (See Chapter 7 for a detailed explanation of the training procedures.)

The coordinator can select anchor papers that seem to represent the various scores on the rubric. These papers should be duplicated for use during the training session. All teachers who are to score papers will meet in one large room. They should be seated with four or five persons at each table. Each reader is given a packet of five or six anchor papers and a copy of the rubric. The coordinator will direct all scorers to read each of the selections in the packet, putting a score on each paper based on the rubric. After most teachers have completed the scoring, the coordinator will call for scores on each paper, noting a central tendency to score the same. A score that is far from the majority score may be discussed. Emphasis is placed on scoring as much alike as possible in order to evaluate the students' writing fairly.

After the training session, the group is ready to begin scoring. Each teacher will be the first reader for a pile of papers; first readers write their scores on the back of the paper. Piles of scored papers are then circulated to the right to receive a second reading; the second reader writes the score on the front of the paper. The third person to receive the stack of papers will examine the two scores on each paper. If the scores are two numbers apart, this scorer will read the paper, giving it a third score. The third reader will cross out the score that appears to be inaccurate and will then add the two remaining scores together and write the student's total score on the top right corner of the front sheet.

Experienced scorers can read from fifteen to twenty papers an hour if student writing is not long. Schedule time according to the total number of papers to be scored. Scoring may take place during the school day if substitutes are available. If scoring is scheduled on Saturday, teachers should expect to be paid for their time.

Report of Scores

The purpose of holistic assessment is to obtain a relatively quick and inexpensive report on writing proficiency across a large student population, usually a school district. The student scores are tallied according to the rubric used. For the nine-point scale, shown in the preceding section, the report of scores for a large urban middle school might look something like this:

Report of Holistic Scoring of Writing Samples: Washington School

Score	Grade 6	Grade 7	Grade 8
9	74	97	112
7	92	115	204
5	121	137	108
3	137	102	48
1	76	54	38
0	7	4	2

Examining the scores reveals that more students are receiving the top score in grade 8 than in grades 6 and 7 (as one would hope). Although the general trend is one of growth, clearly, some students have much to learn. The developmental pattern indicates that writing instruction is more than adequate.

This report can be broken down by schools, and each teacher can receive printouts for the classes he or she teaches. Note that the report of holistic scores across the district does not, however, reveal specific difficulties that students may have.

Individual papers may be returned to students so that they know how their writing ranks compared to that of other students. Students should be encouraged to analyze their own papers, noting how they might improve the writing based on the rubric used for scoring. Many teachers have students use rubrics to score each other's papers occasionally to simulate this kind of holistic scoring. The students learn much about writing as they read each other's work and consider the features of good writing included in the rubric.

PRIMARY TRAIT ASSESSMENT

Primary trait assessment is similar to holistic scoring, but it is more focused. Student writing is scored for one or two traits, for example, tone, organization, or vocabulary appropriate to a given audience. Because one is focusing on a specific trait, the scoring rubric is less complicated, revealing simply the degree to which a trait is present. In districtwide assessment, primary trait scoring is usually used in conjunction with holistic or analytical scoring.

Primary trait scoring is particularly helpful in the classroom for diagnosing student writing abilities. A teacher using primary trait scoring might focus instruction on one aspect of writing that was presented in a more complex holistic scoring rubric. Referring to the rubric presented on page 180, for example, a primary trait rubric might focus on variety of sentence length, thus:

5   Sentence length varies from two to twenty words. Few sentence lengths are exactly the same. The writing provides different pacing and is interesting to read.

3   Sentence lengths vary somewhat, but there are no really complex (long) sentences in contrast to a very short sentence. The writing is rather monotonous and less interesting to read.

1   All sentences are rather short and about the same length. The writing is not very interesting to read.

A student whose writing has been scored using this rubric knows exactly what to do to improve his or her score in terms of sentence length. Intervention lessons on expanding and combining sentences will lead to improved scores based on this rubric. Note that this is a fairly clear aspect of writing for young or less experienced writers to work on. Later, we could discuss more sophisticated matters of style and design rubrics with the students based on, perhaps, development of personification or use of parallelism. A rubric developed for personification might be written, thus:

5   Describes an inanimate object, giving it human characteristics; includes at least five human traits.

3   Describes an inanimate object, giving it some human characteristics; includes fewer than five human traits.

1   Describes an inanimate object, but there is no sense that the object has human traits.

Lessons in which students read literature models of personification or write a collective personification of a chair will assist students in improving their scores on this rubric.
      Primary trait scoring can focus on any one of such varied traits as:

Sustained point of view

Consistency of tense

Correct use of pronouns

Punctuation of dialogue

Meaningful descriptive detail

Coverage of a complete process

Effective use of figurative language

Apt choice of words

Correct use of indentation in dialogue

Support of argument

Fluency of prose

Clear organizational pattern

INTEGRATING EVALUATION INTO THE WRITING PROCESS

As pointed out earlier, evaluation should not be reserved only for writing that has been thoroughly revised, taken through several drafts, and polished for publication (summative evaluation). Nor should evaluation be emphasized only in terms of formal assessment for a school district or the whole state.

Formative evaluation as an ongoing process teaches students more about the writing process than does summative evaluation which results in a grade. Therefore, we need to consider evaluation as a recursive process that begins with the individual's first consideration of topics about which to write, the selection of supportive arguments for an essay, the choice of words from a thesaurus to improve diction, the testing of sentences against his or her ear for language—the full range of writing behaviors—the thinking that permeates the writing process. Evaluation, thus conceived, is an integral part of the thinking processes that writers engage in at all stages of writing.

We need to help students become aware (metacognition) of the evaluative processes that they use without consciously thinking them through. We can discuss the constant need for evaluation, making choices, thinking about what we are writing. Talking about evaluation from this perspective may serve to take away some of the apprehension about evaluation that causes students to worry unduly about writing examinations.

Student Involvement in Evaluation

Students learn how to write by writing, and they also learn how to write by reading. They learn how to write by reading the writing of their peers as well as that of more well-known writers. We can engage students in evaluating writing beginning with their own writing and moving to that of the other students in the class. These evaluation techniques lend a lively stimulus to the composition class, for reading each other's writing is motivating.

Students need intermittent instruction on evaluation. For example, we should introduce a new rubric, talking about the aspect of writing we are teaching. Notice that these techniques are similar to those we presented for editing writing; editing and evaluating writing are inextricably intertwined.

SELF-EVALUATION

The first step for students to follow in evaluating their own writing is to read it aloud sentence by sentence. You may establish the procedure of having students sit at the back of the room facing the wall as they quietly read aloud. Students who are accustomed to this procedure soon ignore students who are at this stage of evaluating their own writing.

Students must be trained to *listen* carefully to their writing as they read aloud. One way of increasing their ability to hear the awkwardnesses in their own writing is to have students record their reading aloud. Then, when they listen to the cassette, they are more likely to notice sentences that need reworking.

Display a checklist based on primary traits on which the class is working to assist students in identifying specific aspects of their writing that are weak. For example, they can literally count the number of words in each sentence or count the number of times they have used the pronoun *I* or the conjunction *and*. Thus, self-evaluation can make use of the same rubrics that we use for peer evaluation or districtwide assessment. At any time, students can see exactly what score (or grade) their writing would receive if another student or the teacher were to evaluate it. And, based on classroom instruction, they should know exactly what they can do to receive a higher score.

PEER EVALUATION

Peer evaluation can follow the same procedures described for self-evaluation. Have students begin working in assigned pairs as they work together to improve each other's writing. You may prepare a step-by-step process they should follow in evaluating their partner's writing, for example:

Step 1: Read the writing aloud slowly. Ask yourself:
Does each sentence flow smoothly?
Are any words left out?
Is the writing interesting?

Step 2: Think about the writing.
Do I understand what _____ is saying?
What else would I like to know?

Step 3: Are there surface mistakes that need correcting?
Can I correct spelling or punctuation?
Can I read the writing easily?

Provide a Reading Response Sheet on which a student reader can record notes and suggestions for changes that their partner might make, thus:

Reader Response Form

Reader_____
Writer_____

Step 1:

Step 2:

Step 3:

After students have worked in pairs successfully, use similar techniques in small groups. Working in groups of four to six, students should respond positively to each student's writing as the writer reads aloud. You might talk with students about appropriate comments they might make. Write ideas on a chart to assist them as they work together:

1. I especially like the sentence _____ because _____
   _____.

2. I like the way you said _____ because _____
   _____.

3. The word _____ is interesting because _____
   _____.

The more ideas they have to work with, the more effective and helpful will be their responses. At this stage, the intent is to engage students in learning to help each other, to enjoy reading each other's work, and to learn more about writing by identifying features of good writing.

Later they can use the Reader Response Form, passing the form with each piece of writing so that several students read and respond to each piece of writing.

As they become more familiar and comfortable with evaluating (editing) each other's writing, they can apply a primary trait rubric, giving each paper an actual score of 5, 3, or 1. Each writer then revises his or her writing, as needed to raise the score.

Move then to using a holistic scoring rubric. Train the students to use the holistic scoring rubric, just as you would a group of teachers. Have them read anchor papers, giving these papers scores. Following is a lesson designed to introduce students to the use of holistic scoring procedures.

A SAMPLE LESSON

TITLE: Holistic Evaluation Techniques

LEVELS: Grades 4–12

OBJECTIVES:

Students will:

1. Compile a list of what makes good writing

2. Compile a list of what makes poor writing

3. Make a judgment about six sample papers

PROCEDURES:

Stimulus

Tell the students to take out a piece of notebook paper. Fold the paper in half lengthwise and label the left column, Good Writing, and the right column, Poor Writing. (Make a similar chart on the board.) Pass out packets of six pieces of writing from which names have been removed.

Activity

Direct the student to read through all of the six samples carefully (allow ten to fifteen minutes). After most have finished reading, have them make their lists of good and poor writing. After five to ten minutes, share ideas to compile class lists on the board.

Now have students give the papers scores ranging from 1–6, with 6 the highest score. Make a scoring chart on the board like the one shown on page 192 on which to record the class scores.

As you call out the scores, students will raise their hands to tell you what score they gave each paper.

Follow-Up

Discuss the procedure and the fact that the scores given were similar.

	1	2	3	4	5	6	
A							
B							
C							
D							
E							
F							

Evaluation

Have students use this scoring procedure with the next set of papers they write.

Teachers who have used holistic scoring with students in their classrooms recommend the following tips:

1. Choose sample papers for training from other classes so students feel free to discuss the work openly.

2. Use code numbers on papers to preserve anonymity.

3. Create a scoring guide appropriate to the kind of writing you are evaluating. Structure criteria to guide students to identify particular qualities you want to stress.

4. For a first experience use only two papers that are widely diverse in quality; later, narrow the gap, challenging students to identify papers scoring closer on a scale.

5. Have students write a score for each paper. Then have them write a justification for each score.

6. Remind students to think in terms of rewarding a paper for what it does well rather than errors made.

7. Tally the votes (as shown in the sample lesson).

8. After discussing the scores given, have students justify the scores given. Try to reach consensus.

9. After most students reach agreement, have them score "live" papers from another class. Later they can score papers from their own class, but proceed slowly.

10. Use separate sheets for each scoring so that students don't know other scores received.

11. As students gain expertise, have them create their own rubrics for scoring.

12. The scores given should be seen as guides for revision rather than grades to be given the papers; students will tend to be more honest in their decisions.

The Role of the Teacher in Evaluation

The teacher plays a major role in evaluation, both in terms of communicating with students and in communicating with parents. At the same time, however, the teacher's role is changing. The good teacher teaches students how to play a more active role in evaluating their own writing and their progress over a period of time. The effective teacher also facilitates student involvement in communicating progress to parents.

COMMUNICATING WITH STUDENTS

Teachers communicate many messages directly to the students they teach—information, evaluation, expectations, and so on. Indirectly, they also communicate attitudes and values, feelings of respect for the students and their work. Establishing a climate of trust and a collaborative workshop atmosphere is important if learning is to take place.

The Writing Workshop

In the classroom that operates as a writing workshop, the teacher is a facilitator. The teacher is also a co-worker who writes along with the students. As a fellow writer, the teacher shares his or her writing with students and talks about problems that arise in writing, such as writer's block.

The ideal classroom arrangement has tables or desks at which students can work individually or in small response groups. A middle school classroom might be arranged something like that shown in Figure 6–1.

In the writing workshop students keep writing notebooks or individual portfolios in which they save all the writing they do over

Figure 6–1. Middle School Classroom Arranged for Collaborative Writing

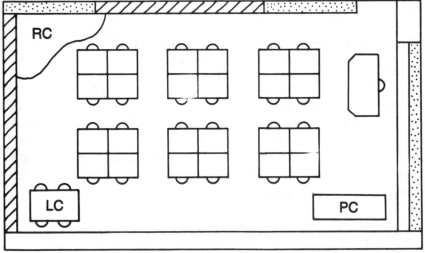

LC—Listening Center
PC—Publishing Center
RC—Reading Center

a period of time. Student portfolios are made of manila folders that can be decorated. The portfolios are stored in a file drawer or a suitable box that will hold a class set.

Students, who are always working on a selected piece of writing, immediately move into the writing mode as they enter the room. Learning in this classroom is less teacher-dominated, with student-writers taking charge of what they are learning. This approach to writing is used successfully in kindergarten as well as college writing laboratories. The teacher-student conference is a natural component of the writing workshop.

Student-Teacher Conferences

Periodically, each student should have an individual conference with the teacher to discuss a specific piece of writing. Students make appointments in advance with the teacher. To take full advantage of their five to ten minutes, they should plan what they want to discuss with the teacher and what they would like to get out of the conference.[6]

Although there are problems involved in setting up conferences, teachers at all levels recommend them highly. Harris notes the following benefits:

1. Stimulates independent learning—the student assumes responsibility for his or her own writing

2. Provides interaction with an experienced reader/writer, the teacher

3. Individualization of instruction—the teacher is talking even for a brief time directly to one student about his or her writing

4. Instruction is directly tied to a specific piece of writing which calls for specific strategies[7]

Studies find that writing really does improve through regularly scheduled individual conferences. The conferences actually save teacher time because teachers can quickly talk about ideas and make suggestions, answering students' questions directly and providing immediate feedback. Talking is much clearer and to the point than the cryptic phrases that teachers often write on student papers. Perhaps one of the most important benefits is the change in student-teacher relationship; a working relationship, a feeling of camaraderie develops as the two writers critique the student's writing together.[8]

As students plan for the conference, they should answer questions discussed in class, for example:

1. What did I learn by writing this paper?

2. What am I trying to say?

3. How can the teacher help me improve my paper?

Fisher and Murray suggest that "The teacher . . . remember his role and not over-teach. It is not his responsibility to correct a paper line by line, to rewrite it until it is his own writing. It is the student's responsibility to improve the paper and the teacher's responsibility to make a few suggestions which may help the student improve it."[9] The teacher's objective should be to encourage students by asking questions that will guide them to become involved with their own writing and then to listen to the students. Students and teachers should work together to evaluate the students' writing—again, the workshop attitude.

Both teacher and student may write comments on a Conference Report Sheet something like this one:

Student-Teacher Conference

Student _____
Teacher _____
Date _____

Student Comments:

What I like most about this paper:

What bothers me most about this paper:

What I tried to improve in this paper:

What I learned from the conference:

Teacher comments about the student's writing:

Suggestions to work on in developing the paper:

COMMUNICATING WITH PARENTS

One of the most effective means of showing parents how their student is performing is through sharing the student's portfolio of writing collected for a full grading period. When conference time is approaching, students should organize their collection of writing, putting it in order, making a Table of Contents, preparing the portfolio for viewing. Students should write a summary of their progress, their accomplishments, and what they have learned about writing for this period of time. This summary might be in the form of a letter to their parents as in this example:

Dear Mom and Dad,

This portfolio holds all of my writing for the third marking period. I think I have really made progress in writing at this time. Mrs. Baker and I agree that I deserve a B in writing based on the writing I have done.

I have learned many new things about writing. I finally learned how to use the dash with a compound appositive. That may not sound very impressive, but I was always puzzled about this kind of punctuation, and now I understand.

The piece of writing that I'm most proud of is my story, "The Little Tin Soldier." It took me almost three weeks to revise the story; every time I read it I make a few more changes. I'm going to send it to *Seventeen* to see if they would consider publishing it. They probably won't, but it's worth a try.

Love,
Nita

Parents will be interested in receiving a report of their student's progress in terms of what objectives the student has accomplished. A checklist like this is helpful both for determining a grade for the student and discussing that grade with students and parents:

Student Progress in Writing

Student _____
Date _____

A. General Organization
The student can write a composition that:
_____ is unified and coherent
_____ contains an introduction, a body, and a conclusion
_____ demonstrates developmental sequence
_____ remains on the topic
_____ includes transitional devices
B. Sentence Structure
The student can:
_____ write complete sentences
_____ avoid run-on sentences
_____ begin sentences in varied ways
_____ vary sentence length
_____ write sentences of varied types: simple, compound, complex, compound/complex
_____ use parallel structures
C. Vocabulary
The student can use:

_____ varied, abundant language
_____ vivid, concrete, sensory language
_____ both figurative and literal language
_____ clear, precise words

D. Grammatical Usage

The student uses:

_____ correct plural forms for nouns
_____ correct verb and auxiliary forms
_____ correct subject and verb agreement
_____ correct pronoun forms

E. Punctuation and Capitalization

The student uses:

_____ appropriate end punctuation
_____ appropriate internal punctuation
_____ capital letters at the beginning of sentences
_____ capital letters for proper nouns

F. Spelling

The student:

_____ generally spells words correctly
_____ uses appropriate tools to correct unfamiliar spellings

G. Revision

The student revises to improve:

_____ organization
_____ content (details, examples, reasons)
_____ appropriateness for audience
_____ style, choice of words
_____ use of conventions

Encourage parents to visit the classroom during writing activities to observe how the process works. Open House meetings provide an opportunity to explain to parents just what you are trying to achieve in writing. If possible, have students participate in conferences and in explaining procedures to parents when they visit the school.

Reflection

Evaluation should be part of the total writing process. A writing program should include both formative and summative evaluation.

The following checklist is useful in assessing how well evaluation is being used within a single classroom or in a school or districtwide writing program.

1. Self-evaluation at each stage in the composing process.

2. Strategies that prepare students to evaluate their own writing.

3. Peer evaluation of each student's writing.

4. Training to enable students to evaluate effectively the writing of their peers.

5. Determination of the purpose of an evaluation effort.

6. Selection of the most appropriate means for conducting an evaluation, for example, holistic, analytical, or primary trait scoring.

7. Policies that reflect consistent and regular assessment of varied writing tasks.

8. The use of student writing samples as a primary means of evaluating student writing.

9. Teacher staff development in the evaluation of student writing.[10]

Challenge

Try these methods of getting started with strategies for evaluating student writing.

1. Work with one or more student writers. Ask them to tell you what a good writer does that makes his or her writing stand out. Together, compile a list of Quality Indicators of Good Writing. Discuss the list with the student(s). Ask how they know this is what good writers do.

   Make a list yourself, adding to the one compiled with the

student(s). This kind of list reveals what you want to teach the students that you work with.

2. Obtain one or more examples of student writing. Apply the Analytical Checklist. Apply one of the Holistic Scoring Rubrics.

3. Write three to five original prompts that you think students would be able to respond to easily.

4. Write a letter to parents, explaining your philosophy of teaching and evaluating student writing. Consider the questions they might ask you to explain.

Endnotes

1. *Notes from the National Testing Network in Writing.* City University of New York, December 1984, pp. 4–6.

2. *Handbook for Planning an Effective Writing Program.* California State Department of Education, 1983, p. 22.

3. *Handbook for Planning an Effective Writing Program,* p. 23.

4. Ibid.

5. Miles Myers. *Procedures for Writing Assessment and Holistic Scoring.* National Council of Teachers of English, 1980, p. 4.

6. Muriel Harris. *Teaching One-to-One: The Writing Conference.* National Council of Teachers of English, pp. 28–35.

7. Ibid., pp. 16–23.

8. *Handbook for Planning an Effective Writing Program,* p. 46.

9. Alan Fisher and Donald Murray. *A Writer Teaches Writing.* Boynton/Cook, 1986, p. 46.

10. *Handbook for Planning an Effective Writing Program*, p. 46.

Exploring Further

Collom, Jack. *Moving Windows: Evaluating the Poetry Children Write*. Teachers and Writers Collaborative, 1985.

Cooper, Charles R. *The Nature and Measurement of Competency in English*. National Council of Teachers of English, 1981.

Cooper, Charles R., and Odell, Lee, eds. *Evaluating Writing: Describing, Measuring, Judging*. National Council of Teachers of English, 1977.

Diedrich, Paul B. *Measuring Growth in English*. National Council of Teachers of English, 1974.

Fagan, William et al. *Measures for Research and Evaluation in the English Language Arts, Volume 2*. ERIC/RCS and NCTE, 1985.

Graves, Donald. Writing: Teachers and Children at Work. Heinemann, 1982.

Greenberg, Karen et al. Writing Assessment. Longman, 1986.

Harris, Muriel. *Teaching One-to-One: The Writing Conference*. National Council of Teachers of English, 1986.

Hillocks, George, Jr. *Research on Written Composition*. ERIC/RCS and National Council of Teachers of English, 1986.

Lundsteen, Sara, ed. *Help for the Teacher of Written Composition (K–9)*. TRIP Booklet, National Council of Teachers of English, 1976.

Reigstad, Thomas, and McAndrew, Donald. *Training Tutors for Writing Conferences*. TRIP Booklet, National Council of Teachers of English, 1984.

Tiedt, Iris M. et al. *Teaching Writing in K-8 Classrooms*. Prentice-Hall, 1983.

7

Taking a Writing Sample in a District: Guidelines

If you can't write it down, you don't have an idea.

Andy Rooney

In this chapter we will go through the procedures that a trainer follows in helping a district take a writing sample for the first time. As discussed in the preceding chapter, we recommend that this kind of writing assessment be scored holistically by the teachers themselves. The teachers should be involved in the entire process of selecting the prompt, developing the rubric, administering the test, and scoring the papers. This experience provides valuable staff development for teachers at all levels of instruction.

Pretend now that you have been asked to conduct a writing assessment for the Holton Elementary School District. (A high school assessment will vary only slightly, as discussed at the end of the chapter.) All students in grades three through eight in the seven schools that comprise the district will participate. Follow the procedures described here. Your superintendent will be very much impressed by your competent handling of this districtwide assessment.

After reading this chapter, you should be able to:

1. Organize holistic scoring for a school or school district

2. Train teachers to read and score student writing samples using holistic techniques

3. Assist a school or district in interpreting scores received by students

4. Prepare a summary analysis of writing scores obtained by all students in a school or district

Making Arrangements for Holistic Assessment

You work begins, of course, before you ever see the teachers in Holton School District. By phone, ascertain the following information:

Number of teachers involved (54)

Number of classes at each grade level (varies)

Number of student papers (1400)

Location of scoring (Holton Jr. High)

Physical set-up of space (Library, 10 tables)

Arrange the scheduling of time required for the assessment. This will probably, although not necessarily, occur in the fall, ideally in early October, a preassessment before teachers have worked with the class for long. Plan two three-hour sessions with the teachers and a date for administering the test, thus:

October 2, Wednesday, 1:00–4:00 All teachers will meet in the library of the junior high school for a planning session.

October 7, Monday The test will be administered in the morning by all elementary school teachers in grades three through six. Junior high school English teachers will administer the test to all students during the day.

October 10, Thursday, 1:00–4:00 All teachers will meet in the library of the junior high school for holistic scoring of writing samples.

Teachers will have to be released for two half-days. Probably school will be dismissed for these periods as in-service days, but that is the responsibility of the school administrator with whom you are working. He or she will also select the room in which you will be working, but do make it clear that the room should be comfortable and large enough to accommodate the number of teachers. Round tables that seat six persons are ideal for the scoring process although square or rectangular tables can be used to seat as many as eight teachers. You will need a chalkboard or an overhead projector as you conduct the planning and scoring sessions.

Plan ahead for the first session. You will need sixty copies (always plan on a few extra) of the materials you need for introducing teachers to the holistic scoring process. The school district will duplicate these sheets for you if you can send the material to them in advance. A full description of the procedures and materials for two workshops to accomplish the preassessment planning and the postassessment scoring of papers follows.

Workshop 1: Planning the Writing Assessment

To conduct this planning workshop, you will need the following:

1. Signs to mark tables by grades

2. Sixty copies of a sheet of sample prompts

3. Sixty copies of a set of Guidelines for Administering the Test

4. Sixty copies of sample rubrics for expository and narrative writing

Examples of these materials are included later in this section.

Arrive early enough to check on the room arrangements and to place markers on the tables according to grade levels, as needed. Have at least one table per grade and two tables marked 3–6 and 7–8 to accommodate the number of teachers who will be attending.

The teachers assemble promptly at 1:00 in an attractive, comfortable library, and you are introduced to them by the assistant superintendent. You smile and murmur a few words about being pleased to have been invited to work with them. Then you begin to work through the procedures. We supply exact words that you can adapt as you wish.

> I'd like to begin by defining our task. (As you speak, you write key words on the board: *Defining Our Task*.)
> First of all, we are planning to evaluate student writing in your district, and I understand that all students in grades three through eight will participate. About fifty-four classes are involved. Is that right?

Defining Our Task

1. Write on the board: *To plan taking a writing sample from all students in grades 3–8*

> First of all, we decided that this writing sample would be scored holistically. I know that many of you are familiar with holistic scoring, but just in case, let's clarify what we mean by this term. The word *holistic* comes from the same Greek root as our English word *whole*. Holistic scoring, therefore, is used to mean scoring a piece of writing by reading it as a whole.
> Holistic scoring can be contrasted to *analytical scoring*, which is a kind of scoring that involves checking all the errors the student makes. This kind of scoring takes a considerable amount of time compared to holistic scoring.
> One of the chief advantages of holistic scoring, then, is that we can score student writing much more quickly. In one afternoon we can score hundreds of student writing samples.
> Another advantage of holistic scoring is that it is positive. When we read a paper holistically, we are assuming that the whole piece of writing has more value than just a summary of its parts.
> Holistic scoring also helps us to clarify our objectives and our expectations for student writing. We'll see how that works as we proceed today.
> Now, let's think about the procedures for conducting this writing assessment to see what we need. First of all, we're going to ask students to write about something—a topic that we all

agree on. Many people refer to this topic as a "prompt," so we need to select a prompt.

Next, we have to consider how we will administer the writing assessment so that everyone will conduct the test the same way. We need a set of Guidelines for Administering the Test.

Last, we'll need a set of criteria by which to judge each student's writing in order to give it a score. We'll set up criteria for each score ranging from 1 to 5. We call this set of criteria a *rubric*. We'll talk more about the rubric in a few minutes.

Our tasks for today, then, include: (1) selecting a prompt, (2) developing a set of guidelines for administering the test, and (3) deciding on a rubric to use in scoring.
(Write on the board.)

    2. Prepare materials for assessment
        a. prompt
        b. guidelines
        c. rubric

SELECTING THE PROMPT

Pass out a copy of sample prompts to all the teachers.

HOLISTIC SCORING MATERIALS I

Sample Prompts

1. This morning when you woke up, you discovered that you were invisible. Tell about your adventures as an invisible person.

2. Who is a special person in your life? What does he or she do for you? Why is he or she special? Describe this person so your friends will know exactly what this person is like.

3. Think back to your first years in school. Tell about something that happened to you that you still remember.

4. Does life sometimes seem mixed-up to you? Write about something that you would like to change in your life.

5. Have you ever been terribly embarrassed? Think about how you felt. Describe what happened to embarrass you.

6. Like most people, you probably enjoy vacations. If you could go anywhere you like, where would you go and what would you do?

7. What is your favorite food? Describe this food so clearly that a reader will want to eat it right away.

8. Imagine that you suddenly met a little man from Mars. Write what you would tell him that would explain how you live.

9. What talent would you especially like to have? Tell what you would do if you had that talent.

10. If you had only one year left to live, what would you do during that year?

This list is a suggestion of prompts. Feel free to adapt these prompts as you design one that you feel all of your students can write on relatively freely. You may also choose to write a completely different prompt after discussing these examples. Your ideas are just as good as anyone's.

Have the teachers discuss the prompts in their small groups for about ten minutes. The purpose is to choose or write a prompt they would like to use for the assessment. Announce when time is almost up and tell the groups that they should make a decision about the prompt they would like to use.

After a few minutes, ask the groups to indicate their choice. Write the choices on the board by number if they come directly from the sheet. If some groups have written different prompts, write those choices in full. Vote on the selections, being sure that newly constructed prompts have a chance to be selected. The prompt that receives a majority vote will be the one used by all classes. Using the same prompt across the district makes assessment of student progress and comparisons more accurate.

GUIDELINES FOR TAKING THE WRITING SAMPLE

Pass out a sample set of Guidelines for Administering the Test. Have teachers read the sheet and recommend changes. Items they usually need to discuss include:

1. Whether to write words on the board during the prewriting discussion

2. The amount of time to take for discussion

3. The specific day and time to administer the test

As you hand out this set of guidelines, make it clear that this is just a sample. Any changes the teachers want to make will be made, and the prompt they have chosen will be inserted. Having the basic work completed, however, facilitates their deciding on how they want to proceed. Again, the final product will be *their* set of guidelines.

HOLISTIC SCORING MATERIALS II

Guidelines for Administering the Test
Taking a Writing Sample

In order to evaluate student writing as accurately as possible, it is important that we all follow the same procedures in collecting a writing sample from our students. In order to achieve this outcome, it is important to follow the steps described.

Prepare a set of writing papers numbered from 1 to 30 (as many as students in your class).

Step 1:   Allow ten to fifteen minutes for oral discussion to introduce the topic, thus:

I want you to think about someone who is special in your life— someone who is really important to you. Close your eyes and picture this person.

Ask several students to name the person they are thinking about. Then ask one student:

Why is _____ really important to you?

Pose the question to others in the same way. Ask:

What does _____ do for you?
What do you especially like about this person?

Do not write words on the board. We want to see how well the students can write by themselves at this stage.

Step 2:   Allow thirty minutes for this part. Explain to the students that they are now going to write about someone who is special in their lives. As you pass out paper, say:

We want to find out how well students in our school write. Other teachers will be reading your writing, so I am giving you a special paper on which to write; you will have a number instead of your name. I'll put your number in my grade book so we can remember it later.
     Today, I want you to write all by yourself, so we can see just how well you can write. Of course, I want you to do your very best, but don't worry about spelling. If you can't spell a word, just do the best you can. Tell your ideas about this special person. Why is the person special to you?

Write the topic on the board:

Who is a special person in your life?
Why is this person special?

Encourage students to continue writing. As they finish, collect the papers and let them read quietly. At the end of thirty minutes, collect all papers, put them in the attached envelope, and send them to the office.

Revise these directions, as the group wishes. The final set of guidelines will be distributed to each teacher before the day the test is to be administered.

PREPARING A SET OF CRITERIA FOR EVALUATION

The final task to be completed is deciding on the criteria or standards (rubric) against which all papers will be judged. Provide a sample for both expository and narrative writing because the prompt will determine the kind of writing produced. The samples facilitate teacher discussion and agreement on criteria they consider realistic for their students.

HOLISTIC SCORING MATERIALS III

Sample Rubrics for Evaluating Student Writing

Sample Rubric for Expository Writing

Score	Characteristics of Writing
5	Writes at least one coherent paragraph on topic
	Includes details and interesting words
	Uses varied sentence structures
	Relatively free from mechanical errors
	Uses transitional devices
	Demonstrates some originality of expression
3	Writes an organized paragraph
	Sticks to the topic in general
	Uses some descriptive words
	Makes few mechanical or spelling errors
1	Writes one sentence or more
	Shows little evidence of paragraph construction
	Makes numerous mechanical and spelling errors
0	Writes little or nothing
	Writes on a different topic

Sample Rubric for Narrative Writing

Score	*Characteristics of Writing*
5	Tells a coherent story Includes descriptive details and interesting words Includes dialogue; uses quotation marks Demonstrates some originality of expression Relatively free from error
3	Tells a simple story Demonstrates a sense of sequence Ideas can be understood Uses some descriptive words Makes some mechanical or spelling errors
1	Writes one sentence or more Ideas can be understood Makes many mechanical and spelling errors
0	Writes little or nothing Writes on a different topic

Encourage the teachers to discuss these sample rubrics in small table groups. Then, with the group as a whole, discuss any recommendations and make the final decisions by voting, as needed.

Teachers may decide to alter the rubric to accommodate varied grade level expectations. They may create one rubric for grades 3–6 and another for grades 7–8. The revised rubric(s) should be duplicated for use in scoring student papers.

The tasks have now been completed. Review the schedule for administering the assessment and remind the teachers that they will receive copies of the guidelines that include the prompt before the test date. You might conclude:

Does anyone have any questions? We've done a good job today. I appreciate your working so hard. I look forward to working with you again when we score the writing papers on _____.

Following this workshop, you will need to see that copies of the revised guidelines are made and distributed to teachers.

Workshop 2: Holistic Scoring

To conduct this scoring workshop, you will need the following:

1. Signs to mark tables by grades

2. Sixty copies of the rubrics for writing

3. Sixty identical packets of student-written papers (to be used for practice)

4. Writing samples of all students to whom test was administered

Arrive about an hour early for the scoring workshop so that arrangements can be made comfortably. Mark the tables by grade levels: 3, 4, 5, 6, 7, 8. Include two tables marked 3–6 and 7–8 to accommodate variation in the number of teachers.

As teachers arrive, direct them to sit at tables with six people at each. (Print directions on board.) When most teachers have arrived and are seated, begin.

> I think we're ready to begin now. As you know, we are going to score your student writing papers today. We prepared a copy of the rubric you decided on for scoring. We will pass them out now so that each of you has a copy. I am also going to give you a packet of student writing papers that we will use for practicing using the rubric.

After everyone has these materials, continue:

> Now I want each one of you to read the first paper in the packet and to decide on a score for that paper. Write the score you choose on the back of the page in the bottom corner.

> Be sure that this procedure is followed precisely, as it is important later.

> How many people gave this paper a 5? a 3? a 1? Most of us agreed on the score for this paper, didn't we?

Now let's see why some of you chose a different score.

Ask a few people to explain and discuss their reasons for choosing a different score. Note that having the criteria defined clearly helps us agree on the score. As individuals, we want to score the papers as everyone else does in order to be fair to the students.

Repeat this procedure with other papers in the packet. If teachers ask about using the scores of 2 or 4 when they can't decide on 1, 3, or 5, tell them that is exactly what they should do.

Collect the packets of practice papers.

We are now ready to work with the whole writing sample. Let me explain exactly what we will be doing before we pass out papers to read. Each paper will be read by two people, so it will receive two scores. We will add those two scores together so that the highest score any student can get is 10.

(Draw table diagram on the board.)

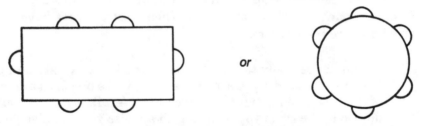

or

Each of you will receive a pile of papers. You will read a paper and write the score on the back of the paper at the bottom, just as we did before. Then you will pass that paper to the person on your right. You will read and score all of the papers you have in your pile.

After you finish reading your papers, you will have another reader's papers accumulating on your left. You will be the second reader for these papers. DO NOT LOOK AT THE SCORE GIVEN BY THE FIRST READER! Read each paper and put your score at the bottom on the *front* of the paper. Again, place the scored papers on your right.

After finishing the second scoring, you will have a pile of fully scored papers on your left. For this third set of papers, your job is to add the two scores together and to write the total score at the top of the student's paper.

When each person has completed the reading of two sets of papers and adding scores for a third set, our job will be finished. Do you see how that will work?

After the papers are scored, we will collect them so we can tally the scores for the district. Afterwards, you will receive the papers for your students.

Before we distribute the papers, I do want to caution you about talking. It is very important that we not talk. It disturbs others and it will delay us in completing the scoring of all the papers. I will be here at this table to answer any questions you may have. If you need to take a break, please step outside.

Distribute the papers by grade levels to the various tables, designating one teacher to divide them up equally among the six readers. As soon as the papers are distributed, teachers should begin reading and scoring.

Collect all scored papers and place them in envelopes by grade levels.

Using Results

Results of the writing assessment should be tallied for the entire district to show parents and school staff the writing performance of students in general. Scores may then be analyzed at the school level to see how schools perform. Then, of course, each teacher should analyze the scores to see how his or her students are performing in general and to diagnose problems at an individual level.

DISTRICTWIDE PERFORMANCE

A secretary can tally student scores on the writing sample. The tally sheet, using the rubric described in this chapter, would be organized, thus:

Writing Assessment Summary

Score	Number of Students by Grade Level					
	3	4	5	6	7	8
10						
9						
8						
7						
6						
5						
4						
3						
2						
1						
0						

This simple tally shows immediately where the students rank by grade level. It provides a picture of writing abilities throughout the district. By examining this chart, one may ascertain the following:

1. The number of students whose scores fall below a middle score of 5: If only a few students fall below the score of 5, for example, the district probably has a satisfactory performance level in the area of writing.

2. Groups of unusually high or low scores: Is one specific teacher affecting the work of his or her students? If students in one class all perform outstandingly well, that teacher must be doing something worth commending and sharing with other teachers. On the other hand, if students in another class have scored consistently low, the teacher may need special help and supervision.

3. Need for staff development: A preponderance of low scores probably indicates that teachers need help in teaching writing more effectively to the students in their classrooms. Certainly priority should be given to improving writing scores gradually over the next few years.

INTERPRETATION AT THE SCHOOL LEVEL

Each school principal will be interested in seeing how students in his or her school performed. Based on the scores, plans can be made with teachers to improve the scores of those who scored low. Certain groups of students may need special help.

Comparisons can be made, of course, among the different schools' performance. Sometimes performance varies distinctly because of the school population which clearly must be taken into account. The principal should discuss the schoolwide writing program with the faculty. Interpreting the results of the assessment together, they should make plans based on what the assessment tells them.

TEACHER USE OF TEST RESULTS

Each teacher is naturally concerned about district and school performance in general. But sixth-grade teacher, Mrs. Bernard, is most concerned about the individual students in her class. Five students write very well, and their test performance demonstrated their ability. Joe, however, who usually writes well, wrote a lifeless little story that scored only 6. Also, there are three children who just arrived from Vietnam, who naturally had trouble writing in English. Mrs.

Bernard will be giving each student's writing careful scrutiny as she determines how best to help each one.

Mrs. Bernard, like all of the teachers involved, will use these writing samples as benchmarks for each student's writing. Copies of the writing samples will be filed in the students' cumulative folders, but copies will also be placed in their portfolios. She will talk with each student to review their performance with them and to make plans for helping them help themselves. These papers and other writing in the portfolio represent important information to share with parents at the first parent-teacher-student conference.

Reflection

In this chapter we have walked through an imaginary Writing Assessment exactly as it would be conducted in a typical elementary school district. This chapter should be useful to anyone who trains teachers in the English language arts or school administrators. Teachers designated as "mentors" or "master teachers" often are called upon to conduct the planning and training that are integral parts of a Holistic Writing Assessment at any level. Adaptations can be made for working with high school districts.

Challenge

These activities will help you get ready to use the ideas described in this chapter.

1. Plan to conduct a Writing Assessment for a local school district. Read the procedures described and prepare copies of the materials used in Workshop 1 and Workshop 2. Conduct the assessment. Note changes you made in the procedures that were helpful.

2. Plan a workshop with your faculty on writing good prompts for students of varying abilities and interests. Talk about

the qualities of a good writing topic. Write sample prompts, share them, and revise them. Create a bank of prompts that all teachers can draw from.

3. Talk with your faculty about using test results. How are they helpful? What practices should be avoided?

Exploring Further

Myers, Miles. *A Procedure for Writing Assessment and Holistic Scoring*. National Council of Teachers of English, 1980.

Tiedt, Iris M. et al. *Teaching Writing in K–8 Classrooms*. Prentice-Hall, 1983. See Chapter 9.

Resources for
Teachers of Writing

*The beautiful part of writing is that you don't have to
get it right the first time, unlike, say, a brain surgeon.
You can always do it better, find the exact word, the
apt phrase, the leaping simile.*

Robert Cormier

This final chapter focuses on extending your knowledge of resources
in the field. Included here are materials that didn't fit into the main
focus of the book yet will be helpful to you. The materials are categorized by the following topics:

Definitions of Terms Related to Writing

Publishing for Teachers

Periodicals That Publish Student Writing

Resource Books for Teachers

Resource Books for Students

Definitions of Terms Related to Writing

We have made no attempt to include every grammatical term that
might be included in a handbook. The terms here are those that
relate directly to writing and that may prove confusing for the students with whom you work.

Abstract

Ideas of a general nature, not concrete, such as liberty, love, or nature. Compare the abstract term, *nature*, with the general term, *forests*, and the specific concrete term, *tree*.

Active (see Voice)

In contrast to passive verbs, active verbs add life to writing.

Ambiguity

Meaning is ambiguous if it can be interpreted in more than one way; for example: Ship sails today.

Analogy

Comparisons based on like features.

Case

The aspect of a noun or pronoun that shows its relationship to other words in a sentence. In English the three cases are subjective (nominative), possessive (genitive), and objective (accusative). For example, the pronoun *he* has the forms of *he, his,* and *him* that are used to make relationships clear.

Coherence

Coherence or cohesion is related to unity. If the parts of a writing selection "hang together," we say it is cohesive. The parts are logically or naturally connected.

Conclusion

The ending of a paragraph, essay, or story. It may be a restatement of the theme or main idea in a paragraph or essay. It presents the solution to the problem or conflict in a story.

Convention

Standards or practices in writing that are generally agreed upon, including punctuation, capitalization, spelling, and certain format features (such as indentation). Conventional practices may be somewhat arbitrary and, therefore, subject to change, but there is usually resistance to changes in conventions.

Diction

Aspects of speaking or writing style that depend on choice of words fall under *diction*, which usually connotes a high level of usage and the effective arrangement, precision, and force of words.

Discourse

Communication of thoughts through use of words in conversation or writing; usually a formal presentation in speech or writing; used in phrase "forms of discourse" to denote types of writing.

Essay

A short, literary prose composition; presents thinking that is usually analytic, speculative, or interpretative. The writer's intent may be to argue or persuade.

Expository Writing

Exposition expounds, sets forth or explains ideas, providing information in terms of examples, definitions, or reasons to substantiate the thesis presented.

Features

Characteristics or traits as in the "features of an essay" or compiling a features list for a specific form of writing.

Generalization

A statement or principle based on inference from examples or facts; inductive thinking.

Grammar

The total structural system of a language that enables native speakers to communicate meaning. This system includes phonology (sounds), morphology (meaningful word forms), and syntax (strings of words we call sentences).

Introduction

The beginning paragraph of an essay that introduces the theme or the first paragraphs of a story that present the characters, setting, and problem. The introduction tells the reader what will follow in the fully developed work.

Mechanics

The routine or technical aspects of writing, usually punctuation and capitalization; the surface features of writing; conventions of writing designed to assist the reader.

Metaphor

Comparison of two unlike things; for example, John is a rock or Time is money.

Mood
In grammar, the attitude of the speaker toward what is being said. Thus, we have sentences that are categorized as declarative (indicative mood), command (imperative mood), or contrary to fact (subjunctive mood). In narrative, mood usually describes the setting or tone in a situation.

Objective
One of the three cases in English, showing a noun's relationship to other words in the sentence. In this case (sometimes called the accusative case), the words are objects of verbs, infinitives, or prepositions. Objective is also used to mean "without bias," as opposed to subjective.

Paragraph
A group of sentences about one topic, usually beginning with a topic sentence, followed by several supportive sentences (evidence, details), and completed with a concluding sentence. Not to be confused with indentation as in "paragraphing."

Parallelism
Use of coordinate forms for coordinate ideas; for example, "I like to fish, to hunt, to explore the countryside." Sometimes achieved through repetition of words and form.

Passive (see Voice)
Most beginning writers should avoid using the passive voice as it tends to deaden writing.

Personification
Giving human attributes to any object or idea; for example, "The balloon smiled as it shook hands with the wind."

Point of View
A stance or way of thinking; an opinion. In narrative, the writer takes a particular stance in telling the story: omniscient (all-knowing; author enters the minds of all characters); limited omniscient (knowing only one mind); objective observer; first person (the author assumes the role of "I").

Repetition
The act of repeating; repetitious usually connotes boring speech or writing. Repetition can be used effectively, however.

Revision

Rereading and editing a first draft until the writing is ready for presenting as a final copy.

Rhetoric

The formal study of the effective use of language. A rhetorical question is one posed for effect with no expectation of an answer.

Scope

The extent or range of coverage; often used in the phrase "scope and sequence."

Sequence

The order in which events occur.

Simile

A comparison of two objects explicitly using the words *like* or *as*, for example, "His voice was like a knife cutting the air."

Style

A composite of the choices a writer makes in expressing ideas effectively—sentence variety, diction, imagery.

Subjective (see **Case**)

A grammatical term; opposite of objective.

Support

Details or evidence used to prove a statement; usually sentences in an expository paragraph.

T-unit

A unit of thought; used in research to identify structural segments usually composed of a subject/predicate construction. One sentence may contain more than one T-unit.

Theme

Subject of discourse, topic; a recurring idea or subject in narrative writing, such as jealousy.

Thesis

A statement of position; often the theme of an essay.

Transition

The change or passage from one position or stage to another; in writing, transitional words or phrases help the reader move smoothly from one passage to another.

Unity
> State of being one unit, a whole; in writing, the components achieve one major effect.

Usage
> Choice of words for effect or based on convention; not the same as grammar.

Voice
> In grammar, an aspect of verbs, as active (the subject acts) or passive (the subject is acted upon). In writing, a stance or position, will or personality, such as to find your "voice."

Publishing for Teachers

In this section we include names and addresses of journals that teachers might send articles to about the teaching of writing or the language arts in general. Included are the major professional organizations in the field that publish a number of journals for specific audiences.

PROFESSIONAL ORGANIZATIONS AND THEIR JOURNALS

> International Listening Association
> Broward Community College, 1000 Coconut Creek Blvd.
> Pompano Beach, FL 33066

> International Reading Association
> 800 Barksdale Rd., Box 8139, Newark, DE 19714-8139
>> Journals: *Reading Teacher, Reading Research*

> National Council of Teachers of English
> 1111 Kenyon Rd., Urbana, IL 61801
>> Journals: *English Journal, Language Arts, English Education*

> Speech Communication Association
> 5105 Backlick Road, No. E, Annandale, VA 22003

SPECIFIC JOURNALS

American Journal of Education, University of Chicago Press
Box 37005, Chicago, IL 60637.

Arizona English Bulletin, University of Arizona
Tucson, AZ 85721.

Bilingual Review, Department of Foreign Languages and
Bilingual Studies, 106 Ford Hall
Eastern Michigan University
Ypsilanti, MI 48197.

California English, Box 4427, Whittier, CA 90607.

California Reader, 3400 Irvine Ave., Suite 118
Newport Beach, CA 92660.

Childhood Education, Association for Childhood Education
International
11141 Georgia Ave., Suite 200, Wheaton, MD 20902.

Contemporary Education, Indiana State University
School of Education, Statesman Towers W., Room 1005
Terre Haute, IN 47809.

Educational Horizons, Pi Lambda Theta, 4101 E. 3rd Street
Bloomington, IN 47401.

The Elementary School Journal, University of Chicago Press
Box 37005, Chicago, IL 60637.

Instructor, 545 Fifth Ave., New York, NY 10017.

The Journal of Negro Education, Box 311
Howard University
Washington, DC 20059.

Mathematics Teacher, National Council of Teachers
of Mathematics, 1906 Association Dr., Reston, VA 22091.

Media and Methods, American Society of Educators
1511 Walnut St., Philadelphia, PA 19102.

Phi Delta Kappan, 8th & Union, Box 789
Bloomington, IN 47402.

School Arts, 50 Portland St., Worcester, MA 01608.

Science and Children, 1742 Connecticut Ave., NW
Washington, DC 10009.

Science Education, 605 3rd Ave., New York, NY 10158.

Social Education, National Council for the Social Studies
3501 Newark St., NW, Washington, DC 20016.

Wilson Library Bulletin, 950 University Ave.
Bronx, NY 10452.

Young Children, National Association for the
Education of Young Children, 1834 Connecticut Ave., NW
Washington, DC 20009.

ADDITIONAL RESOURCES

Jo Bennett. "Getting Your Manuscript into Print." *English Journal*, October 1980.

Stephen Judy, ed. *Publishing in English Education.*
Boynton/Cook, 1982.

Writer's Market. Annual publication by: Writer's Digest
Books, 9933 Alliance Rd., Cincinnati, OH 45242. (Available
in most public libraries.)

Periodicals That Publish Student Writing

Here is a useful list of magazines that publish students' original
writing. Request a copy of the publication's guidelines for specific
information.

Action (ages 12–14)
730 Broadway
New York, NY 10003

Alive! for Young Teens
Box 179
St. Louis, MO 63166

American Girl
830 Third Ave.
New York, NY 10022

Boy's Life (ages 8–13)
1325 Walnut Hill Lane
Irving, TX 75062

Chart Your Course (ages 6–18)
P.O. Box 6448
Mobile, AL 36660

Child Life (ages 7–11)
1100 Waterway Blvd.
P.O. Box 567B
Indianapolis, IN 46206

The Children's Album
P.O. Box 1318
Turlock, CA 95381

Children's Digest (ages 8–10)
address same as *Child Life*

Children's Playmate (ages 3–8)
address same as *Child Life*

Christian Living (ages 15–17)
850 No. Grove Ave.
Elgin, IL 60120

Christian Science Monitor
1 Norway St.
Boston, MA 02115

City Kids (ages 11–14)
1545 Wilcox
Los Angeles, CA 90028

Cobblestone (ages 8–13)
Box 959
Farmingdale, NY 11737

*Cobblestone: The History Magazine
for Young People* (ages 8–14)
20 Grove St.
Peterborough, NH 03458

Cricket (ages 6–12)
Box 2670
Boulder, CO 80321

Current Events
245 Long Hill Rd.
Middletown, CT 06457

Current Science
address same as *Current Events*

District: Young Writers Journal (ages 9–14)
2500 Wisconsin Ave. NW, #549
Washington, D.C. 20007

Dynamite (ages 8–12)
645 Count Morbida's Castle
Marion, OH 43302

Ebony Junior
820 S. Michigan Ave.
Chicago, IL 60605

Electric Company Magazine (ages 6–10)
200 Watt St.
P.O. Box 2923
Boulder, CO 80321

English Journal (ages 12–17)
Arizona State University
Tempe, AZ 85281

The Friend (ages up to 12)
23rd Floor, 50 E. North Temple
Salt Lake City, UT 84150

Fun Publishing Company (grades 1–10)
P.O. Box 40283
Indianapolis, IN 45240

Guideposts (ages 12–18)
747 Third Ave.
New York, NY 11217

Hanging Loose (ages 14–18)
803 Church St.
Honesdale, PA 18431

Health Explorer (ages 9–11)
address same as *Electric Company
Magazine*

Highlights for Children (ages 3–12)
2300 West Fifth Ave.
P.O. Box 269
Columbus, OH 43216

Highwire (ages 12–18)
217 Jackson St.
Lowell, MA 01852

Humpty Dumpty's Magazine (ages 4–6)
Benjamin Franklin Literary
and Medical Society, Inc.
Box 567
1100 Waterway B
Indianapolis, IN 46206

Jack and Jill
Box 567B
Indianapolis, IN 46206

Jr. Medical Detective (ages 10–12)
address same as *Highwire*

Junior Scholastic
50 W. 44th St.
New York, NY 10036

Just About Me (ages 12–19)
247 Marlee Ave., Suite 206
Toronto, Ontario, Canada M6B 4B8

Know Your World
245 Long Hill Rd.
Middletown, CT 06457

Language Arts (for teachers)
Dr. Julie Jensen
414 Sutton Hall
University of Texas
Austin, TX 78712

Merlyn's Pen (grades 7–10)
P.O. Box 716
East Greenwich, RI 02818

Muppet (ages 8–14)
475 Park Ave.
New York, NY 10015

Oasis
Good Apple, Inc.
Box 299
Carthage, IL 62321

Odyssey (ages 10–12)
625 E. St. Paul Ave.
P.O. Box 92788
Milwaukee, WI 53202

Paw Prints (ages 6–14)
National Zoo
Washington, D.C. 20008

Peanut Butter (ages 4–7)
P.O. Box 1925
Marion, OH 43302

Penny Power (ages 9 and up)
256 Washington St.
Mount Vernon, NY 10550

*Program to Recognize Excellence
in Student Literary Magazines*
1111 Kenyon Rd.
Urbana, IL 61801

Purple Cow (ages 12–18)
110 E. Andrews Dr. NW
Atlanta, GA 30305

Ranger Rick
National Wildlife Education
1412 Sixteenth Street NW
Washington, D.C. 20036

Ranger Rick (ages 5–12)
National Wildlife Foundation
17th and M Streets NW
Washington, D.C. 20036

Read (grades 6–9)
address same as *Know Your World*

Scholastic Scope (ages 15–18)
730 Broadway
New York, NY 10003

Scienceland (ages 3–8)
501 Fifth Ave.
New York, NY 10017

Science World (ages 12–16)
730 Broadway
New York, NY 10003

Sesame Street (ages 2–6)
P.O. Box 2895
Boulder, CO 80321

Seventeen (ages 13–21)
850 Third Ave.
New York, NY 10022

Sprint (ages 9–11)
730 Broadway
New York, NY 10003

Stone Soup (ages 4–12)
P.O. Box 83
Santa Cruz, CA 95063

Straight (ages 13–19)
8121 Hamilton Ave.
Cincinnati, OH 45231

The Sunshine News (ages 14–17)
465 King St. East, #14A
Toronto, Ontario, Canada M5A 1L6

Teenage Magazine
217 Jackson St.
P.O. Box 948
Lowell, MA 01853

3-2-1 Contact (ages 8–14)
P.O. Box 2932
Boulder, CO 80321

Voice (ages 12–18)
730 Broadway
New York, NY 10003

Wee Wisdom (ages 6–13)
Unity Village, MO 64065

World (ages 8–12)
National Geographic World
Washington, D.C. 20036

Writer's Update
4812 Folsom Blvd., #250
Sacramento, CA 95819

Writing! (grades 7–12)
P.O. Box 310
Highwood, IL 60040

Young Ambassador
P.O. Box 82808
Lincoln, NE 68501

Young World (ages 10–14)
address same as *Child Life*

Your Big Backyard (ages 3–5)
1412 16th Street NW
Washington, D.C. 20036

Resource Books for Teachers

These titles are directed toward K–12 teachers who are working with young writers in the classroom. They suggest many ideas and techniques for encouraging students to write more effectively. They also provide a theoretical background for accepted approaches to teaching composition today.

Applebee, Arthur. *The Child's Concept of Story: Ages Two to Seventeen.* University of Chicago, 1978.
———. *Writing in the Secondary School: English and the Content Areas.* National Council of Teachers of English, 1981.
Berthoff, Anne E. *Forming-Thinking-Writing: The Composing Imagination.* Hayden, 1978.
———. *The Making of Meaning: Metaphors, Models, and Maxims for Writing Teachers.* Boynton/Cook, 1981.
Camp, Gerald, ed. *Teaching Writing: Essays from the Bay Area Writing Project.* Boynton/Cook, 1983.
Cooper, Charles, and Odell, Lee, eds. *Evaluating Writing: Describing, Measuring, Judging.* National Council of Teachers of English, 1977.
Elbow, Peter. *Writing without Teachers.* Oxford, 1973.
Flower, Linda. *Problem-Solving Strategies for Writing,* 2nd ed. Harcourt, 1985.
Garrison, Roger. *How a Writer Works: Through the Composing Process.* Harper, 1981.
Graves, Donald H. *Writing: Teachers & Children at Work.* Heinemann, 1983.

Grossman, Florence. *Getting from Here to There: Writing and Reading Poetry.* Boynton/Cook, 1982.

Grubb, Mel. *Using Holistic Evaluation.* Glencoe, 1981.

Jensen, Julie, ed. *Composing and Comprehending.* NCRE and NCTE, 1984.

Johnson, Ferne. *Start Early for an Early Start: You and the Young Child.* American Library Association, 1976.

Judy, Stephen N., and Judy, Susan J. *An Introduction to the Teaching of Writing.* Wiley, 1981.

Krashen, Stephen. *Second Language Acquisition and Second Language Learning.* Pergamon, 1981.

Kroll, Barry, and Vann, Roberta. *Exploring Speaking-Writing Relationships: Connections and Contrasts.* NCTE, 1981.

Lawlor, Joseph, ed. *Computers in Composition Instruction.* SWRL Educational Research and Development, 1962.

Loban, Walter. *Language Development: Kindergarten through Grade Twelve.* National Council of Teachers of English, 1976.

Macrorie, Ken. *Searching Writing.* Boynton/Cook, 1984.

McWilliams, Peter A. *The Word Processing Book: A Short Course in Computer Literacy.* Prelude Press, 1982.

Moffett, James, and Wagner, Betty Jane. *Student-Centered Language Arts and Reading, K–13: A Handbook for Teachers,* 3rd ed. Houghton Mifflin, 1983.

Myers, Miles. *A Procedure for Writing Assessment and Holistic Scoring.* National Council of Teachers of English, 1980.

——— and Gray, James, eds. *Theory and Practice in the Teaching of Composition: Processing, Distancing, and Modeling.* NCTE, 1983.

Rico, Gabriele. *Writing the Natural Way.* Tarcher/Houghton Mifflin, 1983.

Schultz, John. *Writing from Start to Finish.* Boynton/Cook, 1982.

Shaughnessy, Mina P. *Errors and Expectations: A Guide for the Teacher of Basic Writing.* Oxford, 1977.

Smith, Frank. *Writing and the Writer.* Holt, 1982.

Stillman, Peter. *Writing Your Way.* Boynton/Cook, 1984.

Strong, William. *Sentence Combining and Paragraph Building.* Random, 1981.

Thaiss, Christopher J., and Suhor, Charles, eds. *Speaking and Writing K–12.* NCTE, 1984.

Tiedt, Iris M. *The Language Arts Handbook.* Prentice-Hall, 1983.

——— et al. *Teaching Writing in K–8 Classrooms.* Prentice-Hall, 1983.

————— et al. *Reading, Thinking, Writing: A Holistic Language and Literacy Program for the K–8 Classroom.* Allyn and Bacon, 1989.

————— et al. *Teaching Thinking in K–12 Classrooms.* Allyn and Bacon, 1989.

Tiedt, Pamela, and Tiedt, Iris. *Multicultural Teaching,* 2nd ed. Allyn and Bacon, 1986.

Tollefson, Stephen K. *Shaping Sentences: Grammar in Context.* Harcourt, 1985.

Turbill, Jan. *No Better Way to Teach Writing.* Primary English Teaching Assn., 1983.

Weaver, Constance. *Grammar for Teachers: Perspectives and Definitions.* National Council of Teachers of English, 1979.

Wresch, William, ed. *The Computer in Composition Instruction, A Writer's Tool.* NCTE, 1984.

Zinsser, William. *Writing with a Word Processor.* Harper, 1983.

Resource Books for Students

Motivate and excite K–12 students about language study by introducing them to books about words and how the English language works. Integrate language information into the writing program. This annotated list includes an indication of the level of difficulty: Primary, Intermediate, or Advanced.

Adams, J. Donald. *The Magic and Mystery of Words.* Holt, 1963. Interesting essays for advanced students; good teacher resource. A

Adler, David A. *Finger Spelling Fun.* Watts, 1980. Good practice for spelling; aids understanding of deaf persons. P-I

—————. *The Carsick Zebra and Other Animal Riddles.* Holiday, 1983. Fun with words. P

Adler, Irving, and Adler, Joyce. *Language and Man.* Day, 1970. Importance of speech and communication. I

Alexander, Arthur. *The Magic of Words.* Prentice-Hall, 1962. Language development. I

Allard, Harry, and Marshall, James. *The Stupids Have a Ball.* Houghton, 1979. Fun with language. P

Applegate, Mauree. *The First Book of Language*. Watts, 1962. Use of parts of speech in writing. I

Ashley, Leonard. *The Wonderful World of Superstition, Prophecy, and Luck*. Dembner, 1984. Discussion of superstition and predicting the future. I

Asimov, Isaac. *Words from the Bible*. Houghton Mifflin. Also: *Words of Mathematics, Words of Science, Words on the Map, Words from the Myths*. Excellent books on the origins and meanings of words. I-A

Basil, Cynthia. *Nailheads and Potato Eyes*. Morrow, 1976. Body parts in language. P

————. *Breakfast in the Afternoon*. Morrow, 1979. Compound words. P

Batchelor, Julie. *Communication: From Cave to Television*. Harcourt, 1953. Explains the ways of communicating. I

Bayer, Jane. *A, My Name Is Alice*. Dial, 1984. Fun with language; great illustrations! I

Bernstein, Joanne. *Fiddle with a Riddle*. Dutton, 1980. Riddles about famous names; treasure hunt with clues. I

Bishop, Ann. *Annie O'Kay's Riddle Round-up*. Dutton, 1982. Fun with language. I

————. *Cleo Patra's Riddle Book*. Dutton, 1982. More fun with language. I

Borgmann, Dmitri A. *Language on Vacation: An Olio of Orthographical Oddities*. Scribner, 1965. For advanced students and teachers. A

Bossom, Naomi. *A Scale Full of Fish and Other Turnabouts*. Greenwillow, 1979. Multiple meanings. P

Bourke, Linda. *Handmade ABC: A Manual Alphabet*. Addison, 1981. Introduction to sign language. I-A

Boynton, Sandra. *A is for ANGRY*. Workman, 1983. An alphabet book that focuses on animals and adjectives. I

Briggs, A. Allen. *The Play of Words*. Harcourt, 1972. An excellent resource for the teacher. A

Brown, Marc. *Spooky Riddles*. Random, 1983. Fun with language. I-A

Burgess, Anthony. *The Land Where the Ice Cream Grows*. Doubleday, 1980. Manipulation of sounds and words. I

Caldwell, John. *Excuses, Excuses: How to Get Out of Practically Anything*. Crowell, 1982. Absurd excuses and illustrations. I

Cataldo, John W. *Words and Calligraphy for Children*. Van Nostrand, 1969. Brings words and art together in exciting ways. I-A

Charlip, Remy et al. *Handtalk: An ABC of Finger Spelling & Sign Language.* Parents, 1974. Wonderfully illustrated introduction to sign and finger spelling; good for understanding deaf persons. P-I-A

Chase, Stuart. *Danger—Men Talking!* Parents, 1969. An introduction to semantics. I

Cole, Babette. *The Slimy Book.* Random, 1986. P

Cole, William, and Thaler, Mike. *Monster Knock Knocks.* Archway, 1983. Word play. I

Corbett, Scott. *Jokes to Read in the Dark.* Dutton, 1980. Fun with language. I-A

Cox, James A. *Put Your Foot in Your Mouth and Other Silly Sayings.* Random, 1980. A book that explains idioms and tells how some of them started. Sam Weissman's cartoon illustrations are funny. May inspire students to research and illustrate their own book of idioms. I

———. *Jokes to Tell Your Worst Enemy.* Dutton, 1984. More fun with language. I

Davidson, Jessica. *The Square Root of Tuesday.* McCall, 1969. Logic. I

———. *What I Tell You Three Times Is True.* McCall, 1970. Information about language including ideas about semantics. I

———. *Is That Mother in the Bottle? Where Language Came From and Where It Is Going.* Watts, 1972. Short chapters on various aspects of language. I-A

———. *How to Improve Your Grammar.* Watts, 1980. An overview of prescriptive grammar including usage. I

———. *How to Improve Your Spelling and Vocabulary.* Watts, 1980. Provides information about spelling and language. I

Denison, Carol. *Passwords to Peoples.* Dodd, 1956. Entertaining introduction to history of language. I

DeVane, Lenchen. *The Adventures of Tony, David, and Marc.* Exposition, 1976. ABC vocabulary book with information about word origins. I

Dohan, Mary Helen. *Our Own Words.* Knopf, 1974. Interesting information for the teacher. A

Dugan, William. *How Our Alphabet Grew.* Golden, 1972. Information about the letters of the alphabet. I

Elting, Mary, and Folsom, Michael. *Q Is for Duck.* Houghton, 1980. An alphabet guessing game, and an ABC book to add to your collection. "A is for zoo. Why? Because . . . animals live in the zoo." A class book would be fun to make using this pattern: "S is for Amy, because she is smart." I

Epstein, Samuel, and Epstein, Beryl. *The First Book of Words.*
Watts, 1954. Beginning study of language. I. Also: *The First
Book of Printing.* Watts, 1955. I

Ernst, Margaret. *Words.* Knopf, 1936. Development of the English
language. I

————. *More about Words.* Knopf, 1951. An assortment of stories
about words origins. I

————. *Words: English Roots and How They Grow.* Knopf, 1954.
Origins of English words. I

Espy, Willard R. *A Children's Almanac of Words at Play.* Potter,
1982. Fun with language; good ideas for teachers. I-A. Look
for adult books by Espy, for example: *An Almanac of Words at
Play* and *Have a Word on Me.*

Esterer, Arnulf K., and Esterer, Louise A. *Saying It Without Words.*
Messner, 1980. Using signs and symbols to communicate. I

Fadiman, Clifton. *Wally the Wordworm.* Macmillan, 1964. Wally's
adventures as he eats his way through the dictionary. P-I

Farb, Peter. *Word Play: What Happens When People Talk.* Knopf,
1974. Good resource for teachers. A

Ferguson, Charles. *Say It with Words.* University of Nebraska, 1959.
Background for teachers. A

————. *The Abecedarian Book.* Little, 1964. Clever observations
about words. I-A

Fisher, Leonard E. *Alphabet Art: 13 ABCs from Around the World.*
Four Winds, 1978. Comparative study. I

Folsom, Franklin. *The Language Book.* Grosset, 1963. Explores all
aspects of language development. I

Foster, G. Allen. *Communication: From Primitive Tom-toms to Tel-
star.* Criterion, 1965. Presents various ways of communicating.
I

Frasconi, Antonio. *See and Say: Guarda e Parla; Mira y Hable; Re-
garde et Parle: A Picture Book in Four Languages.* Harcourt,
1955. Cross-cultural study. I

Friend, M. Newton. *Words: Tricks and Traditions.* Scribner 1957.
Introduction to word play. I

Funk, Charles. *Hog on Ice and Other Curious Expressions.* Harper,
1948. More about words in our language. I

————. *Thereby Hangs a Tale.* Harper, 1950. Exploration of cliches
and idioms of English. I

————. *Heavens to Betsy.* Harper, 1955. Humorous explanations of
curious expressions. I

Funk, Charles E., Funk, Charles E., Jr. *Horsefeathers and Other
Curious Expressions.* Harper, 1958. Word origins. I

Funk, Wilfred. *Word Origins and Their Romantic Stories*. Grosset, 1950. An excellent resource; includes affixes derived from both Greek and Latin. I-A

Garrison, Webb. *What's in a Word?* Abingdon, 1965. Origins of words. A

Gasiorowicz, Nina, and Gasiorowicz, Cathy. *The Mime Alphabet Book*. Lerner, 1974. Acting out words. P-I

Gomez, Victoria. *Wags to Witches: More Jokes, Riddles and Puns*. Lothrop, 1982. Fun with language. I

Gounaud, Karen Jo. *A Very Mice Joke Book*. Houghton, 1982. Funny mouse names. I

Greenfeld, Howard. *Sumer Is Icumen In*. Crown, 1978. Information about how language changes. I

Gwynne, Fred. *The Sixteen Hand Horse*. Windmill, 1980. Hilarious book illustrating homonyms and figures of speech. It is exactly like his two previous books: *The King Who Rained* and *Chocolate Moose* published in 1970. Easy to motivate children to make figures of speech books. P-I

Hanlon, Emily. *How a Horse Grew Hoarse on the Site Where He Sighted a Bare Bear*. Delacorte, 1976. Fun with homonyms. P-I

Hansen, Carl F. et al. *A Handbook for Young Writers*. Prentice-Hall, 1965. Handbook covering grammar and usage. I

Hanson, Joan. *Antonyms*. Lerner, 1972. P

———. *Homographs*. Lerner, 1972. P

———. *Homonyms*. Lerner, 1972.

———. *Synonyms*. Lerner, 1972. P

Hautzig, Esther. *At Home: A Visit in Four Languages*. Macmillan, 1968. Introduces children to French, Spanish, and Russian; good for multicultural teaching. P-I. Also: *In School* and *In the Park*.

Helfman, Elizabeth. *Signs and Symbols Around the World*. Lothrop, 1967. Use of written language to communicate. I

Hill, Donna. *Ms. Glee Was Waiting*. Atheneum, 1979. All kinds of excuses. P

Hofsinde, Robert. *Indian Sign Languages*. Morrow, 1956. Presents Indian "vocabulary." I

Hogben, Lancelot. *Wonderful World of Communication*. Garden City, 1959. History of communication. I-A

Hoguet, Susan R. *I Unpacked My Grandmother's Trunk*. Unusual ABC: acrobat, ben, cloud . . . zebra. Dutton, 1983. I

Holt, Alfred H. *Phrase and Word Origins*. Dover, 1961. Interesting information about history of language. A

Holzer, Hans. *Word Play*. Strawberry Hill Press (616 44th Avenue, San Francisco CA 94121), 1978. Humorous definitions add interest to the study of words. A

Hook, J. N. *The Story of American English*. Harcourt, 1972. Good background for the teacher. A

Hooks, William et al. *Read-A-Rebus*. Random, 1986. Fun with word play. I

Hudson, Peggy, comp. *Words to the Wise*. Scholastic, 1971. Paperback about words. I

Hunt, Bernice. *The Whatchmacallit Book*. Putnam, 1976. Vocabulary development. I

Hymes, Lucia, and Hymes, James M. *Oodles of Noodles*. Scott, Foresman, 1964. Introduction to word play. P

Irwin, Keith G. *The Romance of Writing*. Viking, 1957. Early developments of writing. A

Jacobs, Frank. *Alvin Steadfast on Vernacular Island*. Dial, 1965. Fun with words in a fictional context. I

Janeczko, Paul B. *Loads of Codes and Secret Ciphers*. Macmillan, 1984. Ideas for using and breaking codes. I

Johnson, Wendell S. *Words, Things, and Celebrations*. Harcourt, 1972. Useful information for the teacher. A

Juster, Norton. *The Phantom Tollbooth*. Epstein/Random, 1961. Fiction that presents many concepts about words and the dictionary. I

Katan, Norma Jean, and Mintz, Barbara. *Hieroglyphs: The Writing of Ancient Egypt*. Antheneum, 1981. Combines language study with history. I-A

Kaufman, Joel. *The Golden Happy Book of Words*. Golden, 1963. Introduces many words. P

Keller, Charles. *Smokey the Shark*. Prentice, 1982. A very funny collection of jokes, riddles, and puns. I

———. *Norma Lee, I Don't Knock on Doors: Knock, Knock Jokes*. Prentice, 1983. Word play. I

Kohn, Bernice. *What a Funny Thing to Say!* Dial, 1974. Discusses modern usage, for example, slang and jargon. I-A

Kraske, Robert. *The Story of the Dictionary*. Harcourt, 1975. Dictionary-making and the great lexicographers. I-A

Laird, Charlton. *Thinking about Language*. Holt, 1964. Discussion of words, grammar, and man's use of language in society. A

———, and Laird, Helene. *Tree of Language*. World, 1957. Development of the English language. I

Lamb, Geoffrey. *Secret Writing Tricks*. Nelson, 1975. Fun with codes and other language activities. I

Lambert, Eloise. *Our Language*. Lothrop, 1955. History of English.
I

———, and Pei, Mario. *Our Names: Where They Came from and What They Mean*. Lothrop, 1960. Exploration of names. I

Lipton, James. *An Exaltation of Larks*. Grossman, 1968. Focuses on collective nouns. A

Maestro, Betsy, and Maestro, Guilio. *Traffic: A Book of Opposites*. Crown, 1981. Opposites used in sentences. P

Marzollo, Jean. *The Rebus Treasury*. Metheun, 1986. A form of word play children enjoy. I

Mathews, Mitford M. *American Words*. World, 1959. Origins of words. I-A

Merriam, Eve. *A Gaggle of Geese*. Knopf, 1960. Explores unusual words for groups of things. P-I

———. *What Can You Do with a Pocket?* Knopf, 1963. P-I

———. *What's in the Middle of a Riddle?* Knopf, 1964. I

———. *AB to ZOGG: A Lexicon for Science-Fiction and Fantasy Readers*. Atheneum, 1977. A spoof for fantasy lovers. I-A

Michel, Anna. *The Story of Nim: The Chimp Who Learned Language*. Knopf, 1980. Interesting nonfiction; photographs. I-A

Moorhouse, Alfred C. *The Triumph of the Alphabet: A History of Writing*. Abelard, 1953. The story of writing. I-A

Morris, William, and Morris, Mary. *Dictionary of American Word Origins*. Harper, 1963. Up-to-date words and their origins. I-A

Nilsen, Don L., and Nilsen, Alleen P. *Language Play: An Introduction to Linguistics*. Newbury, 1978. Good resource for teachers. A

Ober, J. Hambleton. *Writing: Man's Great Invention*. Peabody Institute, 1965. History of writing. I-A

Ogg, Oscar. *The Twenty-Six Letters*. Crowell, 1948. History of writing. I

O'Neill, Mary. *Hailstones and Halibut Bones*. Doubleday, 1961. Wonderful poems about colors that provides models for children's writing. Available on 2 short films (Sterling). I

———. *Words Words Words*. Doubleday, 1966. Rhymes about sounds and words. I

Opie, Iona, and Opie, Peter. *The Lore and Language of Schoolchildren*. Oxford, 1967. Good resource for teacher. A

Osmond, Edward. *From Drumbeat to Tickertape*. Criterion, 1960. Development of writing and printing techniques. I

Palmer, Robin. *A Dictionary of Mythical Places*. Walck, 1975. A useful book for a unit on myths. I-A

Parish, Peggy. *Amelia Bedelia*. Harper, 1963. One of series; fiction about humorous maid who interprets language literally. P-I
——. *Amelia Bedelia and the Baby*. Greenwillow, 1982. P-I
Partridge, Eric. *A Charm of Words*. Hamilton, 1960. Stories about words. I
Pei, Mario. *All about Language*. Lippincott, 1954. I-A
——. *Our National Heritage*. Houghton, 1965. Cultural and linguistic heritage of Americans. I-A
Perl, Lila. *Candles, Cakes, and Donkey Tails*. Houghton, 1984. Birthday traditions, symbols, and celebrations. I
Provensen, Alice, and Provensen, Martin. *Karen's Opposites*. Golden, 1963. Introduction to antonyms. P
Radlauer, Ruth S. *Good Times with Words*. Melmont, 1963. Using varied words in creative writing. I
Rand, Ann, and Rand, Paul. *Sparkle and Spin*. Harcourt, 1957. Enjoying words together; excellent illustrations. P
Raskin, Ellen. *The Mysterious Disappearance of Leon (I Mean Noel)*. Dutton, 1971. Fiction with a word puzzle. I
Reid, Alastair. *Ounce, Dice, Trice*. Little, 1958. Introduction to word play by an imaginative collector of words. I
Rogers, Frances. *Painted Rock to Printed Page*. Lippincott, 1960. How writing developed from primitive efforts. I
Roget, Peter M. *New Roget's Thesaurus of the English Language*. Rev. by Norman Lewis. Putnam, 1961. An excellent edition of the famous thesaurus. I-A
Rossner, Judith. *What Kind of Feet Does a Bear Have?* Bobbs, 1963. Introduction to word play. P
Russell, Solveig P. *A Is for Apple and Why*. Abingdon, 1959. How our alphabet developed. I
Sage, Michael. *Words Inside Words*. Lippincott, 1961. Stresses enjoyment of words. I
Sarnoff, Jane, and Ruffins, Reynold. *Words: A Book about the Origins of Everyday Words and Phrases*. Scribner, 1981. Introduction to etymology. I
Scarry, Richard. *Early Words*. Random, 1976. A book for preschool and early reading. P
——. *My First Word Book*. Random, 1986. P
Scheier, Michael, and Frankel, Julie. *The Whole Mirth Catalog*. Watts, 1979. Humorous ways of working with language. A
Schultz, Sam. *101 Monster Jokes*. Lerner, 1983. Funny jokes and riddles. I

Schwartz, Alvin. *A Twister of Twists, A Tangler of Tongues*. Lippincott, 1972. A fascinating collection of twisters from different languages. I

———. *Tomfoolery: Trickery and Foolery with Words*. Lippincott, 1973. New and old tricks that students enjoy. I-A

———. *Witcracks: Jokes and Jests from American Folklore*. Lippincott, 1973. A humorous approach to language study. I

———. *Ten Copycats in a Boat and Other Riddles*. Harper, 1980. Riddles from folklore. I

———. *The Cat's Elbow and Other Secret Languages*. Farrar, 1982. Describes 13 different secret codes or languages beginning with Pig Latin. I

———. *Scary Stories to Tell in the Dark*. Lippincott, 1982. Also: *More Scary Stories to Tell in the Dark*. Lippincott, 1983. Stories often told as part of our folklore. I

Scott, Joseph, and Scott, Lenore. *Hieroglyphs: Your Own Secret Code Language*. Van Nostrand, 1974. Encoding-decoding. I

Segal, Joyce. *It's Time to Go to Bed*. Doubleday, 1980. Creative excuses. P-I

Severn, Bill. *People Words*. Washburn, 1966. Word origins. I-A

———. *Place Words*. Washburn, 1969. Word origins. I-A

Shipley, Joseph T. *Playing with Words*. Prentice-Hall, 1960. Written for adults; provocative for advanced students. I-A

———. *Word Games for Play and Power*. Prentice-Hall, 1962. A second book about word play and the fascination of words. I-A

Sparke, William. *Story of the English Language*. Abelard, 1965. The development of the English language. I

Sperling, Susan Kelz. *Poplollies and Bellibones: A Celebration of Lost Words*. Penguin, 1979. The author explains and defines English words from the 17th century and before. Students could use these unusual words in their stories and poetry. I-A

Steig, William. *CDC?* Farrar, 1984. Fun with letters that make words. I-A

Stevenson, James. *Clams Can't Sing*. Greenwillow, 1980. I

Supraner, Robyn. *Giggly-Wiggly, Snickety-Snick*. Parents, 1978. Textures. P

Tripp, Wallace, comp. *Marguerite, Go Wash Your Feet*. Houghton, 1985. I

Vasilu. *The Most Beautiful Word*. Day, 1970. Search ends with discovery; stimulates discussion. P

Waller, Leslie. *Our American Language*. Holt, 1960. Introduction to the story of English. P

White, Mary S. *Word Twins*. Abingdon, 1961. Homonym fun. P

Williams, Kit. *Masquerade*. Schocken, 1980. Verbal and visual riddles. I

Wiseman, Bernard. *Morris Has a Cold*. Dodd, 1979. Fun with language. P

Yates, Elizabeth. *Someday You'll Write*. Dutton, 1962. Specific information for the young writer on plot development and so on. I

Zim, Herbert S. *Codes and Secret Writing*. Morrow, 1948. Fascinating language activities. I

Index